Experienc
Green ...

by
Rob Hardy & Teresa Moorey

www.capallbann.co.uk

Experiencing the Green Man

Cover design by Paul Mason

Published by:

Capall Bann Publishing
Auton Farm
Milverton
Somerset
TA4 1NE

1

Contents

Spring Maiden 1997

Spring Maiden by Jane Brideson

Acknowledgements

Many thanks to Jane Brideson for her wonderful artwork. Jane's work can be purchased - please see the contact details in the appendix.

Thanks also to Dave and Sue James for their valuable photographic contributions, and to Rob's wife Janet for hers - and for her patience.

Thanks to June Cook for Teresa's picture

Also by Teresa Moorey, publishd by Capall Bann:

The Moon and You
The Magic and Mystery of Trees
In Search of Pagan Gods
Astrology For Lovers

Wheel of the Year (with Jane Brideson)

Chapter One

Finding the Greenman

'My eyes mist over, green it seems,
Roots break through my chest, to me.
My face unfolds to receive the Sun
They buried me under an acorn
to the sound of muffled drum.
One hundred years later we are one.'

Who is the Greenman?

The Greenman is a figure of a human head carved in stone or
wood, part of his features made from living vegetation. His
image is bewitching, conveying a subtle power. He gives the
impression that he shares a strange symbiosis with the plant
life of the land, especially with trees. This mysterious masked
foliate face that peeps out of the sacred forest of our dreams,
is known by the name: "The Greenman". While his image is
rooted in a time before time, the name itself is new. It was
the late Kathleen Basford that coined the term in her book
'The Greenman' (Brewer 1978), listed in the Bibliography. He
is also known by a host of different names. In Great Britain
he has been known as Foliate head, Jack in the green. To the
French he is known as Masque feuilles 'leaf mask'. In similar
fashion the Germans called him ' blattmaske' which has the
same translation 'leaf mask'. However, today he is generally
known simply as 'The Greenman'.

Green Man

Casual observers may dismiss him as just another gargoyle, but the Greenman is so much more than that and his symbolism is very powerful. The Greenman is almost definitely a pre-Christian icon. This being the case, today he is dubbed with the general term 'pagan symbol'. These strange sculptured masks are found in many churches and cathedrals, worked in the main in stone by the stone mason. However they can be found carved in wood or depicted in paint or even stained glass windows.

The sculptural features of the Greenman

He is certainly represented in many different ways and sometimes it may be hard to decide whether an example qualifies as a true Greenman. For instance, if you were looking in your local church for images of the Greenman and came upon a statue of a figure holding a sprig of oak in one hand, would that qualify him as a Greenman? One person might say yes, another might say no. However, the location where he was discovered in the church should be noted, for future reference. The general rule of thumb here is quite simple - if he looks like a Greenman then he probably is!

The Greenman falls into three main categories of common foliage mask.

1: The first type is a human head surrounded by leaves.

2: In the second type, the mask head is surrounded by leaves as in the first example, but in this case the face itself is partly made up of sculptured leaves.

3: A third example is similar to the second but this time the vegetation or branches grow out of the mouth. In some rare examples vegetation can be seen growing out of the eyes as well as the mouth.

Tewkesbury Abbey Gate

Finding the Greenman

'Where can I find the Green King?
East of the Moon and west of the stars.'

The Greenman can be found in countless churches and
Cathedrals across the length and breadth of Europe, and also
Asia, from the humblest chapel in Scotland through highly
decorated churches in Moscow to New Delhi temples on the
Indian sub-continent. You can find him staring down from the
lofty roof spaces adorning a delicate carved boss where the
arching wooden beams intersect, or straining under the
weight of a stone corbel. He can also be found under images
of the virgin and child, lending his stout strength, forged in
the heart of ancient oaks, to the new mother and babe.
Similarly you may also discover him carved in stone over a
doorway or window, keeping guard. Clearly, you could find the
Greenman almost anywhere in the church. On the other
hand you may not find him at all! Not all churches are home
to the Greenman, although you can never be sure without an
extensive search. The Greenman has a habit of taking you by
surprise!

Your local church may well have some interesting examples of
the foliate mask, and this is the first place to check. Other
well-known places to go a-hunting in the British Isles include
Rosslyn Chapel, south of Edinburgh in Scotland, Fountains
Abbey, North Yorkshire, St Mary's Nantwich in Cheshire,
Kilpeck Church in Herefordshire, Southwell Minster,
Nottinghamshire, St Laurence Ludlow in Shropshire,
Tewkesbury Abbey, Gloucestershire, Bristol Cathedral, and
St. Mary Redcliffe in Bristol. Some of these we look at more
closely in Chapter Seven. Stained glass Greenmen appear in
Notre Dame de Paris, the Greenman guards the Buddha in
the temple of Swayambunath, in Nepal and appears in many
places, even woven into baskets, in the Apo Kayan sector of
Borneo. It is probable that the Greenman, in some guise, is

8

Tewkesbury Abbey

Green Woman

found worldwide, for he is testimony to the life-force within nature.

Looking outside churches and cathedrals

In recent years, Greenman masks have started to appear on public buildings and taverns, establishing a refreshing trend. Indeed, many private dwellings now also sport Greenman sculpture. You can buy a stone replica of the Greenman from one of the many New-Age shops, which have become popular since the boom in pagan merchandise. Most of the examples we have encountered in these shops tend to be on the smaller scale, though if you travel to your local garden centre, you will be able to purchase larger examples sold as garden ornaments. As well as the three dimensional type, there are countless images of the Greenman in picture form in books and magazines. As we become increasingly alienated from the natural world in our concrete ghettos, so the Greenman image becomes more fascinating, more sacred and more compelling

However, the true, magical image of the Greenman can be glimpsed peeping from a tangled thicket in park or garden. You may meet him out in the wide places high on the moors, embodied in an ancient tree shaped and twisted into fantastic contortions by the winds and storms. Look for old oak men outlined against bleak horizons. Or deep in the bewitched woodland where the scent of the trees finds its way into our very bones, here the greenman moves with each stir of the branches or shift of the light.

Finding Green Women

There are countless numbers of female figures carved into the fabric of church art. They are usually seen carrying fruit, or woven into a general wooden decoration that may be found around the church. Heads of women may be seen crowned with vegetation, fruit, or both. Many may be dismissed, as

11

heads of angels. Some however, could be figures of goddesses associated with the land. The classical goddesses Flora or Demeter, spring to mind - 'Demeter' quite literally means 'Earth Mother', the Greek goddess of nature and the land, while Flora was the Roman goddess of flourishing springtime. Flora had her own priesthood (the Flamen) who led her followers in her festival to praise the fruit blossom, flowers and the vine. The 'Floralia' was celebrated from the 28 April until the 3 May. It must be remembered that such goddesses, in more ancient times were not ornamental consorts to powerful male gods but awesome creatrix figures that were demoted, in the classical era, to a more subservient role. The Greenwoman is probably not precisely a Goddess, as the Greenman is not quite a god (although more of this later). They are more of an example of a primal epiphany of the life force in the world of vegetation, animistic and perhaps pantheistic rather than polytheistic.

When searching for the 'pure' Greenwoman it can be valuable to look anew at any female figures portrayed in the church that do not seem to be goddesses or angels, as they could well be Green women. In our practice session we shall be reminding you to take notes, these will help you get a total picture.

Christianity, paganism and the Greenman

Some historians believe that in the past the church did its utmost to sweep paganism from Europe. However they did not have things all their own way in this respect. It was not easy to convert the local community, who for the most part could not read or write, and even if they were not completely illiterate would not have been able to read the Bible or even understand the priest. The ceremony of worship according to prescribed forms was both written and spoken in Latin. However, the people were no doubt in awe of this new

Pew end at Crowcombe Church, Somerset

religion, and Christianity won many converts. Despite this we have little doubt that there persisted a hard core of the people who felt uncomfortable with it. The old religion that Christianity was slowly to usurp had grown up out of the land; stone and river, hill and dale; blade of grass and mighty tree. The new religion was not interested in the earth, it looked all the time to heaven and to a promised Afterlife, awaiting the obedient and just.

Before the Industrial Revolution folk lived close to the land. This largely agricultural community marked the stations of the changing seasons with their own brand of local festivals, celebrating the return of spring, bringing in a successful harvest etc. These things brought comfort and reason to their world. They felt at home with the old ways and would return to them, time and time again in one form or another.

The Church was not slow to realise this and tried to curb what they saw as the worst of the pagan practises. Furthermore, they tried, whenever possible, to replace them with their own Christian doctrine. This worked well, as different regions across Europe had their own gods and practices, and many different ways of celebrating the turning seasons of the year. Pagan folk were, for the most part, fairly accepting, and tended to look for similarities in ways of worship. Christianity linked them all together and brought stability by adding a certain amount of its teachings. Communities continued to hold their own pagan festivals, and many of these found their way under the umbrella of Christianity. It is probable that the Church was prepared to adopt a certain amount of pagan symbolism into places of worship, possibly to appease the local community. And perhaps there was a sneaking fear that they might 'throw the baby out with the bath water'! Either way, perhaps they decided to take out a little 'magical insurance', and as a result incorporated a certain amount of pagan art into the fabric of their churches.

The builders who worked on the construction of those magnificent testimonials to the power of Christ, lived in an age where being a Christian was a far different prospect then it would be in today's modern society. The idea that the Christian God was the only God would have seemed an alien concept to them. They might have believed that the son of God of the new testament was the most powerful God. But it seems doubtful that village people believed that he was the only God. In fact many of the early grass roots Christians were both practising pagans and Christians at one and the same time - furthermore, they felt comfortable with both. Christianity and the old ways were blurred around the edges.

It is also worth noting that masons, in those days, held a certain amount of power. Because of their skill and indispensability in the process of erecting places of worship, there may have been a limit to what the priest could control – a master-mason was not to be found around every corner! It has been suggested that much wisdom about architecture and its power to influence the human spirit was brought back to Europe from the Holy Land by the Knights Templar. This is believed by some to have been guarded by masons, part of whose tradition has come down to us in the modern practice of Freemasonry. Possibly there is more in the heritage of the Greenman than simple nature-worship, perhaps he was the literal 'figure-head' for the pseudo religious practises of a secret society of masons jealously guarding their knowledge.

More examples of the Greenman
Not all Churches have images of the Greenman, but a surprising number do. There are some famous examples, including for instance Exeter Cathedral which sports not just one, but some twenty Greenman masks. Curiously early churches, especially those built before the reign of James I, are more likely to have incorporated into their fabric images of the Greenman. These pre James I churches, were predominately built on old pagan sites, ancient groves, stone

circles or sacred mounds. This practice had two main purposes. Initially, it deprived the local people of their place of spiritual focus, and furthermore showed the local people (in what some feel was the most callous way) that Christianity had power over ancient belief because it could destroy traditional places of worship. Another factor, of course, is that if a church were to be erected on the site, say, of an old sacred grove, people would be in the habit of coming to that spot for their religious observance, so their routine would remain much the same. In the same way the Church took over many of the old festival dates – e.g. Halloween (Samhain)– making them part of the Church calendar, 'All Saints Eve'.

These actions are depicted symbolically in the icon of George and the dragon. St George represents Christianity in its evangelistic warrior guise. The dragon on the other hand represents the coils of 'earth energy' that underpin and unite the ancient pagan sites. So, put simply, your mound is the sleeping coiled dragon, and St George is symbolic of the church built on it, in an attempt at suppression. Moreover in all the images of St George and the Dragon we have seen, St George appears to wound the dragon, not kill him. St James' in the town of Dursley, Gloucestershire has a beautiful stained glass window picturing George and the Dragon, illustrating this.

St George also appears as one of the main characters in the rural mummers plays. In some parts of the country he appears as himself. However in other versions, he is played by a leaf-covered young man known as 'Green George'. It is certain that George was associated with the colour green, traditionally. For example it is recorded that a large sum of money was spent dressing him in a mantle of green satin, in Norwich in 1492. Furthermore as the hero of the Gloucestershire mummer play (covered fully in Chapter Three), he undergoes death and resurrection at the winter solstice - so perhaps it is truly the spirit of the Greenman,

St George and a dragon

St George and a dragon

stirring the Dragon from its sleep dressed up in the guise of
St George. The symbolism here is complex, for the name
'George' is itself linked to the earth and the ancient goddess
Ge which is a form of Gaia (Earth). An early Greek goddess.
Gaea or Gaia was credited with creating the universe and the
first race of gods.

While George may be depicted fighting the dragon, he is also
an embodiment himself, of the raw power of the earth, in a
more conscious and differentiated guise.

However through one way or another, the spirit of those old
sacred sites found its way into the churches that were built
over them. The mask of the Greenman which represents
man's link with mother earth, is one good example. These
early churches offer great hunting grounds for Greenman
iconography and evidence of pagan influence in general.

It is great fun to explore your local church to see if you can
find any images of the Greeman. Besides your notepad, also
take your camera with you when out 'hunting'. You will need
a telescopic lens and a powerful flash gun, as many of the
images are high up in the fabric of the ceiling structures.

Is the Greenman the devil?

It is worth noting that in the bible there is no description of
the Devil. The popular image of the Devil today is a semi
human figure with cloven hooves, forked tail, horns and a
'goatee' beard, plus a lustful grin! It now seems obvious that
this character was modelled from the classical goat foot god;
'Pan', who was half man, half goat. Pan was not demonic but
in fact was a god of the flocks and fertility, generally believed
beneficial to the community. Later the gods of the old religion
become the Devils of the new. However, Pan's image, for
reasons presumably best known to the early Church fathers,
was transferred onto the Christian devil. Strangely, the

*A devilish Green Man
on a Story-telling bench, Gloucester*

Church has made no attempt to demonise the Greenman. Yet nevertheless, some of the Greenman masks look malevolent with tongue protruding and eyes popping out. Other examples of his effigy are treated in a more sympathetic way. Consequently the human representation of the image may be sad and reflective, seeming to show concern for the human condition. So it seems unlikely that the Greenman has anything to do with the Devil, whatever or whoever he may be.

As a matter of interest the modern pagan movement which has taken the Greenman so much to its heart, claims not to believe in the devil as such, arguing that the devil is a Christian divinity essential to its dualistic theology concerning heaven and hell. It therefore has nothing to do with modern paganism.

Is the Greenman a God?

We looked briefly at possible divine aspects of the Greenman in the passage on Greenwomen. The Greenman most certainly could have been a pre-Christian God of the forests. In the past, trees covered most of Europe in a blanket of green. Folk who lived within their shadows may well have perceived the face of a god among the foliage. But if this was the case, no firm evidence has been found in the writings of early historians, or religious artefacts to support the idea that the Greenman was a God. There are many pagan gods of classical times which share strong similarities with the Greenman, but these are distinctly different to the more savage Greenman image, as they grew up out of the tame pastoral landscape of southern Europe that bordered the Mediterranean sea. Our well-known Greenman is characteristic of the robust nature of the dark forests of northern Europe. We shall be looking further at this in chapter two. The fact remains, it is unlikely that the Greenman was a god in the sense that we understand the term today. However the enigma that surrounds the Greenman certainly gives him the quality of divinity.

Shamanism and the Greenman

It is more likely that the Greenman has links with shamanism than that he may be a god or devil. A Shaman is a type of witch doctor, a magical priest able to travel into the spirit worlds to seek out wisdom and bring healing, for the good of the tribe. The name itself comes from the cold Scandinavian lands and derives from the Tungusic word 'Saman' which may in turn be derived from the Vedic 'sram' which means 'to heat oneself or practice austerities. In the bleak frozen Northern lands nomadic tribes followed the herds of reindeer which roamed far and wide in search of food. These people were renowned for their shamans and magicians. Lapland shamans were credited with the power to restore life to dead animals, by using just their bones. All tribal peoples have one thing in common, they live in a twilight world of myth and dreams. Their culture arises from a rich font of folklore, myth and legend. Stories told about the heroic deeds of their ancestors around their communal fires on long winter nights are as real to them, as the solidity of the television sitting in the corner of the room is to you or me! Some might indeed say that what appears in the TV screen is harder to believe! The Shaman's special gift is his ability to move between the every day world of his people, and the world of myth and magic that underpins his universe. This is achieved through the medium of self-induced trance, usually to the beat of a drum, which is, of course, made partly from wood. He is usually helped by the powers he draws from his totem animal, and the adept use of hallucinogenic drugs found in the local flora and fauna. Once in a trance he steps into the spirit world and climbs the 'World Tree'

The idea of the 'World Tree' is and was a way of 'mapping' the subtle realms. Upper World is in the branches, Middle World

Tortworth Chestnut

is represented by the trunk and Lower World by the roots. Upper World is the realm of angelic and god-like figures, Middle World is similar to our everyday world, but also contains the spirits that walk alongside us, unseen. Lower World is a subterranean power-house, where dwell ancestral spirits and race memories. The shaman travels all these worlds in search of the wisdom needed for the tribe. The fact that these are structured on a tree form suggests that the natural world and the spirit world are one – it is a holistic view. It also suggests that there may be a magical quality to trees themselves, acting as portals to other dimensions.

Once at the top of this great Tree, the shaman is in a position to help the tribe with the insight gained in his shamanic journey. The world tree or in some cases the 'axis mundi' world pole, is central to European shamanic practises. The image conjured up in the mind's eye of a shaman sitting in the topmost branches of the world tree, his old face peering through the leaves reminds one irresistibly of the Greenman.

The legend of Robin Hood may have concealed shamanic references. Robin himself would have made a good contendor as a shamanic magician, living deep in Sherwood forest, dressed in green, reputed to be the son of Herne the Hunter and spiritual leader of his arboreal outlaw tribe. So it could be argued, that the Greenman could be a race memory of some form of forest shaman, who lived in the seemingly endless broad leafed forests of northern Europe, acting as a shepherd of both trees and man.

The Druids also would doubtless have had a deep understanding of the Oak groves they venerated. Interestingly, one meaning of the word Druid is 'Oak man'.
In James G Frazer's celebrated masterpiece: 'The Golden Bough' 1922, (see Bibliography) he writes about Rex Nemorensis (King of the Wood). Here was a priest-cum-shaman whose duty it was to protect a sacred tree that stood

in the centre of a region dedicated to the Goddess Diana, called Nemi (Diana's mirror). The story goes that if a runaway slave could successfully snap off one of the tree's boughs, he won the right to fight the priestly guardian in single combat - and the fight would be to the death. If the slave was victorious he would then rule in his stead, thus becoming the new guardian , with the title 'Rex Nemorensis' (King of the Wood). The broken branch was known as the Golden Bough. It is clear in this story that both combatants were a human sacrifice to the tree, and the sacred ground it stood upon - one man offering up his life's blood to nourish its roots, the other his days and nights for its protection. The story of Rex Nemorensis, is echoed in the death and resurrection plays that are still performed in Britain today, the mummer's plays being a good example. Rex Nemorensis could also be the Green Man, or one contender for the title.

Practice Session

Making contact with the Greenman

Gaining insight into the ancient and mysterious Greenman is much more than an intellectual exercise. There are two principle ways you may discover him – the practical, external way and the abstract – but very vivid – inner way. For your first exploration, start with the practical.

Seeking out the Greenman

If you have an interest in the Greenman your first port of call is your local church – if you have not visited it already. Go with a pencil, notebook and camera, preferably with a zoom lens. Make notes of where you find the Greenman but also jot down how he makes you feel, what you think of this particular image, why might he be sited in this specific spot etc. You may like to start a scrapbook containing your notes, photographs, any literature about the locality, sketches – in short, anything you feel is relevant.

If however you are unlucky with your search for greenmen in your local churches try your nearest Cathedral. Once there, don't be afraid to ask someone if there are any Greenmen sculptures or any art forms that represent foliage. There is always someone keeping an eye on the public and you will find they are often only too willing to help you.

Whether or not you find your Greenman locally you are sure to want to venture further afield to discover as many representations as you can. Why not make the Greenman an object of outings, or even a pilgrimage? The Greenman can be an inspiration for holidays and trips.

Green Woman

Spirit of Bacchus - Top
Drunken Baccus - Bottom

By Robert Hardy

Chapter Two

The Greenman and the Old Gods

Many God-forms

In ancient groves haunted by the mysterious hooded figures of the Druid priesthood the Greenman was king. Many gods partake of the Greenman image. Odin, for instance, chief of the Scandinavian gods, has important connections with trees. Legend states that he hung on the Scandinavian World Tree, Yggdrasil, until the secrets of the runes came to him in a shamanic revelation – we met the concept of the World Tree in the previous chapter. Although Odin was a warrior god his connection with a great tree is powerful. His German counterpart was Wotan, his Anglo-Saxon Woden – these were creator gods and very potent within their pantheons.

Celtic knowledge in pre-Christian times was passed by word of mouth, so it is hard to be sure of many details. It seems that the Celts had a Horned God of the animals and the woods – this god has come down to us with the names Herne and Cernunnos. This wild, chthonic figure both rules Nature and is an expression of her, in her benign, awesome and also ruthless guises. While this god does not appear to have any specific connection with a tree, or foliage, he is accepted as a god of the forests. Notably he was featured in a TV rendering of the Robin Hood legend, made in the 1980s, as Robin's spiritual guide and mentor.

In addition, there are countless dying and resurrecting vegetation gods, from many parts of the world. Their 'sacrifice' – usually at the sorrowing behest, or at the very least, the knowledge, of their consort, the Great Nature Goddess - represents the eternal cycle of Nature, where things must die in order for new life to be born. Assyro-Babylonian Tammuz is one well-known example. He was lover of the great goddess Inanna, who journeyed to the Underworld to redeem him, in one version of the myth. The ubiquitous image of the Greenman can be discerned in so many myths.

God of mirth and revelry

The Greenman also has a most benign and indulgent aspect. In ancient times, if you travelled south to the Italy, the jewel of the Mediterranean and then took a walk through the pastoral fields, gardens and vineyards of ancient Rome, there you would find them lovingly tended by the citizens – who were all too aware of the presence of the gods.

The gods were not just providers of sustenance and protection to these people but also a source of recreation, and religious inspiration. They wished to be one with their gods through their association with the land, which to them was inhabited by nymphs and fauns and all manner of various mythological, semi-divine nature spirits. These beliefs show through clearly in Bacchanalian rites, held to honour wine and the holy grapevine. At the heart of these rites the Greenman was there, wreathed in grape leaves in the guise of Bacchus the Roman god of wine. With Nymphs and satyrs for his guards he would appear in the centre of his followers, riding on a milk-white ass, leading a wild drunken orgy, to celebrate the bringing in of the grape harvest.

We have here a clue as to why the Greenman has been able to survive, alive and well, into the Twenty First century. He seems to have the power to free people from the every day round of family and work. Freedom to be wild is the buzz word, unrestrained by sexual morality. To put it another way, if you welcome the Greenman into your life he will show you how to blow off some steam now and then and have a little fun! It is probably true that those who are not able to do this once in a while, who cannot give way to a little 'madness' may be the very ones who risk going truly mad!

The ancient Greeks also had a similar God of the vine in their mythology, Dionysus. He was in many ways akin to Bacchus, but with a darker side to his rites. At the Bacchanalian rites the maenads, the women who followed Dionysus on his travels, were said to tear wild beasts apart in mad frenzy, yet on the other hand the maenads showed great gentleness towards young animals. In the Dionysiac cult the rending and eating of raw flesh is probably founded on straightforward magic presumption: 'you become one with the godhead by devouring god in one of his manifestations'. This idea continues in the Catholic practice of taking the body and blood of Christ in bread and wine, in Holy Communion. There are also accounts that in the early Dionysiac mysteries cults his women followers would daub their faces with red wine, and wear beards made of leaves. In contrast men would wear masks of women painted ghostly white with blood red lips. The symbolism of this may be seen as deep and complex, but a simple interpretation is that when we leave ordinary consciousness we encounter different aspects of our personality, including our internal contra-sexual element.

Of course the Greenman is not specifically Dionysus or Bacchus, but there is a definite conceptual link. However, he is not just representative of the God of the grapevine, but of all vegetation particularly the trees of the wood and forests. The Greenman is the link between man and nature he is the very embodiment of the spirit of the wild wood. The idea that trees have a spirit dwelling inside them to some people might be a difficult concept to come to terms with. Tree dwelling

Uley Tumulus, Hettey Peglars Tump, Glos.
Believed to be a Ley-line marker.

spirits are still given religious respect by peoples in some remote areas of the world even today. This belief however would have been commonplace to our pagan forefathers who were no doubt closer to nature and felt divinity in all its aspects and elements. If you, in this day and age, were to stand in some hidden dell by the side of a rock-pool into which cascaded a shining waterfall, you might say: "Can you feel the atmosphere" or perhaps: "Can you feel the spirit of the place" Our ancestors would have gone one step further, giving the spirit of the place a name and an image that was fitting to the mood of the locality. For example, our waterfall might remind our ancestor of a young woman. Furthermore a fitting name could have arisen such as "Dancing laugher" to represent the way the water moved and sounded. So now the spirit of the waterfall takes shape as young water nymph called "Dancing laugher" with the propensity of laugher and dancing! It is easy to see how this works. But we must bear in mind that our ancestors may have been sensing something very real, and quite probably had a clearer image of the natural world than we do, today.

Certain places vital to the well being of the local community, wells and springs would have been regarded as especially holy. The plant kingdom was perceived in a similar way too. The biggest of plants were the trees and the strongest of the trees were the Oak and Yew. For instance, let us imagine a grove of oak trees, planted at a site of special beauty or power. Five hundred years later the power of the spirit of the place would be awesome, having grown with the trees, and the persona of the place would be that of the Greenman residing in the lap of Mother Earth.

Long Barrow, Coaley Picnic Site, Glos

Ley - line marker

Practice Session

1 The Greenman further afield

Having searched the interior of selected churches, as suggested in the Practice Session after in Chapter One, put on your walking boots and explore the woods fields and parks of your neighbourhood. Look for enchanted spots where you can feel the spirit of the Greenman. Returning to your church, examine also the graveyard for images of the Greenman. Furthermore look at the setting of the church. Might it be built on a sacred site, or grove? How does it strike you, instinctively? You may also like to research local records. Explore around the graveyard for ancient yews or any trees of special interest. Make notes.

2 Ley lines

Alfred Watkins was the first to discover the phenomenon of ley lines. He published his theory in a book called: 'Early British Track-ways' in 1922. It was received badly by archaeologists at the time. In 1925 Watkins published 'The Old Straight Track' (see Further Reading for this and other books on the subject) and invites his readers to prove his theories for themselves by using the same methods he had used, the simplest of which you can easily try.

To track these fascinating lines you will need a local Ordnance Survey map, which will show many places of interest. It will indicate local prominent features such as schools, churches, river-fords and bridges, pubs, standing stones, mounds, tors, forts, castles, ancient long barrows and round barrows. Using these features marked on the map you can search for ley lines. The better your knowledge of the countryside the more easily will you be able to locate places of special interest and their straight line formations. One method of identifying them is simply to look on your map for features that line up in a

Chair from the church at Flet Bowter, Somerset

37

Kilpeck Church - top

St Mary Redcliff Church, Bristol - bottom

straight row - for instance a church, a prominent hill, a long barrow, another church and so forth. Take a clear plastic ruler and place your rule through these features and draw a line with a pencil. You will be amazed just how many sites line up.

Ley lines have been described as ancient straight tracks that criss-cross the landscape. The theory is that special landscape features arrange themselves along these mysterious lines, and that places of worship were purposely located there. It has been speculated that churches built on these ancient track ways would have probably been built over pre-Christian holy sites, so making them prime hunting grounds for the Greenman, in spirit and in masonry. Many theories have been put forward as to what ley lines truly are, one of them being that these are lines of 'earth energy' where the power within the earth flows its strongest. Some researchers have noticed that there are more hauntings and supernatural phenomena along ley lines. Find out for yourself!

3 Making true contact with the Greenman a pathworking

Gaining insight into the ancient and mysterious Greenman is much more than an intellectual exercise. There are two principle ways you may discover him – the practical, external way and the abstract – but very vivid – inner way. By far the most impressive way to visit the Greenman is by finding him within. So you may now like to try a guided meditation or path working on the theme of a Bacchanalian rite to tune your mind into the ancient group soul of humanity. In this way a bridge may be formed between ancient and modern rituals, thought patterns and beliefs.

Meditation is a word that is used to cover several types of mental exercise. Really the meditative state is not mysterious. If you can recall that drifting, abstracted mood we all go into at times, looking at a patch of sunlight or candle flame, 'staring into space' you will come close to knowing about the state of mind you need for meditation.

There are many different ways of meditating. Moreover there are as many religious doctrines connected to these meditation techniques. But don't worry - all you need to know at this stage is that meditation falls into too two basic types.

The first is passive meditation much used in Eastern techniques. The objective here is to clear the mind of all thought in order to attain transcendence so that one can become one with the universe and find inner peace. To help the student to clear their mind, the conscious mind is given something to focus on. For example, a candle flame, or a mantra [from the Sanskrit, instrument of thought, from man 'think'] A mantra is a verse, word or sound repeated over and over again to aid concentration in meditation. The way it works is simply by giving the conscious mind something to focus on, in order to allow the sub-conscious and super-conscious to rise to manifest.

The second technique is called active meditation. This technique leads the conscious mind on a journey full of colour and strange symbolism. This in turn excites the sub-conscious, which calls to the super conscious bringing both to the surface. Active meditation is used widely in path workings and guided meditations.

(The super-conscious may be described as the part of your being some would call your soul. It is that essence of yourself that cannot die. It's the reality underlying the phenomenon of all phenomena).

Relaxing to begin meditation
Before you start a meditation or path working you need to be relaxed. Tension in the mind and body is the principle barrier

between us, and the great sea of magical energy that surrounds us, so it is important firstly, to learn to banish tension.

Because we are creatures of habit, your attempts at relaxation will be far more successful if you devote some regular time to them. Ten minutes a day is worth much more than an hour a week. Choose a time when you are most likely to be peaceful and uninterrupted and start your relaxation on your bed, because that will immediately suggest to your unconscious mind that you are going to relax. Later, as you become successful, you may find it better to relax elsewhere, to prevent falling asleep.

Some people favour the method of tensing each muscle in turn, going systematically through the body, tensing and relaxing, and there is some organic merit in this. Others favour visualisations such as warm water flowing over the body carrying away all the cares. Or imagine that all the muscles are powered by little men who are downing tools and walking off. Whatever method you choose, practice it regularly and you will soon be primed to relax quickly, at will. If you have never tried this sort of exercise before it is a good idea to practice relaxing for at least a week before progressing to guided meditation, but this is your choice and you will know best as you come to recognise your responses.

Bacchus pathworking

Having learnt to relax, you will need a quiet, warm room to settle for your pathworking. You could do this outdoors if you prefer - the important thing is you don't want to be disturbed half way through your meditation.

Sit on the floor in a crossed leg fashion with your hands resting on your legs. If you find it difficult to sit on the floor use a comfy seat with a straight back. Close your eyes, breathe deeply and rhythmically until all mental chatter disappears and your mind is clear of thought.

Then imagine you are standing in a large vineyard. It is early morning and the sun is just rising and trying to break through the mist that shrouds the vines. Each vine supports bunches of numerous newly formed green polyps no bigger than blackcurrants. Begin to wander through the vines, feeling mesmerized by the quiet beauty of the palace. Suddenly the mist completely envelops you and you feel a rushing sensation. The mist clears, the atmosphere is hot and all around you people in brightly-coloured costumes are collecting ripe bunches of grapes from the vines and putting them into their baskets. Take your time to observe all of this. Then, after a while, again you are enveloped in a blur of colour and time has moved on once more.

You now find yourself outside a Roman villa, painted white and reflecting the heat of the sun. Many people are seated at long trestle tables. There is a great feast in progress to celebrate the completion of the grape harvest. Part of the celebrations feature praise to the god of the wine Bacchus. Watch what is happening. When everybody has had enough to eat the serious drinking starts, and there is merriment and revelry. After some while a man you know to be the head of the household appears, dressed up as the God Bacchus and seated on a donkey. The younger men and women of the estate escort him and the donkey around the grounds. As the party becomes more outrageously drunk the portly middle-aged man sitting on the donkey, lustily downing a flagon of wine, seems to metamorphose into Bacchus himself.

Turning his head he looks straight into your eyes. How do you feel? How does he truly appear to you? What is his glance telling you? Take your time with this. After a moment, with a laugh and a wink he turns back to his revels. Pause at this point for a moment, savouring what is going on around you – what do you notice?

And now once more for a second the world seems to spin and all is a blur of rushing colours. You open your eyes and you're out of the trance. Thank the god Bacchus for his blessing and take a little food and drink to ground yourself and sprinkle some of the earth in thanks and blessing. Now make a note of all you saw and experienced, for you have been in the presence of the Greenman, in one of his guises, for a precious moment.

Jack In The Green, Bristol

Chapter Three

The Greenman and Folk Customs

Many folk customs can be seen as featuring the Greenman in various guises. These events can be more meaningful – and more fun – if their real meaning of honouring the spirit of life within Nature is appreciated.

Mummers Plays

Let us return you to the Mummers Plays that we mentioned briefly in chapter one. Through our research we feel that the spirit of the Greenman has emerged in the persona of some of the characters acted out in the various Mummers plays performed up and down the country, St George and Father Christmas in particular.

The play we would like to use as an example is performed in around Dursley in the county of Glocestershire. We witnessed the spectacle of the local Mummers Play on the green in front of St James Church in Dursley town centre. This particular group is called: `The Watery Bottom Mummers, They take their name from a small Hamlet situated between Dursley and its neighbouring market town, `Wotton under Edge'. The reason they chose not to name themselves after either Dursley or Wotton under Edge was because they would not get a particularly good reception in the rival town. In Watery Bottom, few residents have loyalties to either town, so everybody is happy!

People from Dursley used to collect water cress from the streams that give Watery Bottom its name. If they walked straight out of the town, cut up through the woods and down the other side into a hidden valley it would take them right into the heart of Watery Bottom. If you travel by the road that skirts the hills you go miles out of your way. Local tradition has it that the Water Cress was cleaner in Watery Bottom then the Water Cress found in the streams that flow around Dursley, this might have been true due to the mills that used the local water in the cloth trade. Probably it was more likely that parents used it as an excuse to get away from the kids on a Sunday afternoon and go for a pleasant walk through some of the best country side in Gloucestershire.

Back to the mummers themselves. The Watery Bottom Mummers visit all the pubs in Dursley and Wotton under Edge, on and around the time of the Winter Solstice. After each performance the Landlord will fill up their wassailing Bowl which the Players pass around between them. In years past, the money they collected they would keep for themselves, today the money collected goes to local charities.

But to celebrate the spirit of the Mummer's play we slightly rewrote the Watery Bottom's play and along with like minded friends performed it at the Pagan Federation annual convention in London.

There are many versions of the same basic Mummers play. Here is the one we uesd for the PF convention. We are sure it will interest you, please feel free to use it if you wish – it is great fun to perform.

Mummers Play

Enter the Green King:

"A room a room, a room, cries I!
In come I your old green king, welcome in or welcome not.
I hope your old green king, will never be forgot.
Yule tide comes but once a year, but when it comes it brings
good cheer, roast beef, and plum pudding make you happy
and sing, but money in the pocket is a mighty fine thing.
And if you don't believe what i say, step in mother christmas
and clear the way".

Enter Old Mother Christmas:

"In comes I, old mother Christmas, under me arm I carries
me basket, in me basket I carries me pegs, in me pocket, I
drops me brass. and I think me self a jolly old lass. on this
merry christmas tide, give me and my players room to
rhyme, and we will show you a jolly good time.
Activity of youth, activity of age, I'll show you the best
activity that's shown on common stage.
if you don't believe what I say, step in King George and clear
the way"

Enter King George:

"In comes I King George, that noble champion bold, and
with my glittering sword, I won five crowns of gold.
T'was I that fought the fiery dragon and brought him to the
slaughter.

And by those means, I also won the king of Egypt's
daughter.
I've travelled all the world around and around, but a man
equal to me never have I found.

Show me the man that before me can stand, and I'll cut him down with sword in hand".

Green King:

"A room, a room, a room, cries I. Lets have bold slasher in this way"

Enter Bold Slasher:

"In comes I, bold slasher is my name and fighting King George is my game, I fought the swords of all the nations, and I'll fight King George with all his proud boastation's, I'll cut him up as small as flies, and send him to Mother Christmas to make mince pies".

All the company join in with:

"Mince pies hot, mince pies cold, let your battle be short and bold".

There now follows a mock battle with wooden swords, George eventually wins and the Bold Slasher lies face up on the floor.

Mother Christmas says:

" Oh King George what hast thou done?
Thou's gone and killed my only son, mine only son, mine only heir, how can'st thou see him bleeding there".

The Green King calls for a doctor. [when playing the pubs, a local doctors name is useD, which adds to the fun]

A room, a room, a room cries I, lets have the Doctor in this way".

Enter the Doctor:

"In comes I, a noble doctor, both stout and good.
And with my hand I'll purge his blood.

I'll give him pills to cure all ills, the itch the stitch, the palsy and the gout, all pains within and pains without, if the old man's in, I'll fetch him out.

Bring me an old woman of seven years dead, eight years buried, nine years laid in her grave, I'll give her one of my pills and maintain her life to be saved.

If there's any can do more then that, let him walk in".

Green King:

"A room, a room, a room cries I, lets have toss pot in this way".

Toss pot

"See! in comes I, the man as ain't been yet, with my great big head and little wit, my heads so big and my wit's so small, but I'll endeavour to please you all. I'm a man of noble vain, I can cure more than thee or any other man".

Doctor:
"What can'st thou cure".

Toss Pot:
" I can cure a magpie with a tooth ache"

Doctor:
"How dost that".

Toss Pot:

"Cut off his head and cook him in cider"

Doctor:

"Yes, sure cure, sure cure"

Doctor:

"Where did'st learn all that?".

Toss Pot:

"I travelled for it".

Doctor:

"Where did you travel".

Toss Pot:

"I travelled round Italy, Spitally, France and Spain, all around england and back again".

Doctor:

"Well cure this poor man".

Toss Pot kneels down and gives Bold Slasher a bottle to drink saying:

"Here Jack! Take a little of this bottle. and let it run down thy throttle, and if thou art not entirely slain, rise up and fight again".

Doctor:

"Thou silly fool, that's no cure. you never knew a doctor to take a small job in hand. but what he made a long'n of it.

But I've got another bottle in my pocket called elecampane.

That will bring a dead man to life again.

Get this flip flop down your chip chop.

A little to his eye a little to his thigh a little to the string bone of his heart rise up bold slasher and play your part"

Slasher recovers, exit doctor.

Bold Slasher:

"King George a mortal man that lives by bread? What makes your nose so long and red".

King George:

"Thou silly fool dost thou not know?

Tis whitbread ale that is so stale, that keeps my nose from looking pale"

(Again the name of the Ale is changed to the beer that is served in the particular pub)

Slasher:

"Fool thou sayest"?

King George:

"What I say I mean".

The two start fighting again.

Green king:

"Charge! peace, put up your swords, you must obey for you will fight another day".

Horned King:

"A room, a room, a room cry I, lets have devil doubt in this way".

Devil Doubt:

"In comes I little Devil Doubt, if you don't give me money I'll sweep you all out. Money I want and money I crave, if you don't give me money, I'll sweep you all to your grave. If this pan could speak he'd say throw in your money right away".

(Little Devil doubt is the coiner, and comes in with a broom)

Green King:

"A room, a room, a room cries I, lets have old Beelzbub in this way".

Beelzebub:

"In comes I Beelzebub and over my me shoulder I carry me club, and in my hand a dripping pan, don't you think I'm a jolly old man. The jolliest man you ever have seen, I carry the word from coven thirteen?

A selection of masks as used in Mummers Plays

We don't come to your town to beg or borrow, to conjure up storms and blight your tomorrows.

We come to your door from the goddess divine, to drive away sorrow, ill feeling and pain.

The whole company:

"With your pockets full of money, and your cellars full of beer, we wish you a happy yule tide and a happy New Year".

The blessing brings an end of the mummers play the Landlord then fills up the Wassail bowl, it is then passed around the players then around the bar for everyone to drink. So doing they shout "Drink Hail". The Mummer would then sing a Wassail song (Waes-Hail translated means (Be thou whole). Here is a good example of a Gloucestershire Wassail song:

"Wassail, Wassail, all over the town!
Our bread it is white, and our ale it is brown,
Our bowl it is made of the white maple tree;
With a wassailing bowl we'll drink to thee.

So here is to the Cherry and to his right cheek,
Pray God send our master a good piece of beef,
And a good piece of beef that we all may see;
With a Wassailing bowl we'll drink to thee.

And here is to Dobbin and to his right eye,
Pray God send our master a good Christmas pie,
And a good piece of pie that may we all see;
With a wassailing bowl we'll drink to thee.

So here to the Broad May and to her broad horn,
May god send our master a good crop of corn,
And a good crop of corn that may we all see;
With a Wassailing bowl we'll drink to thee.

And here is to Fillpail and to her left ear,
Pray God send our master a happy New Year,
And a happy New Year as e'er he did see;
With our wassailing bowl we'll drink to thee.

And here is to Colly and to her long tail,
Pray God send our master he never may fail
A bowl of strong beer; I pray you draw near,
And a jolly wassail it's then you shall hear.

Come landlord fill us a bowl of your best,
Then we hope that your soul in heaven may rest;
But if you draw us a bowl of the small,
Then down will go Landlord, bowl and all.

Then here's to the maid in lily white smock,
Who tripped to the door and slipped back the lock!
Who tripped to the door and pulled back the pin,
For to let these jolly wassailers in".

(Cherry and Dobbin are horses
Broad May, Fillpail and Colly are cows)

With the above players with their spoken parts there is also a
Dragon and a white horses skull with a snapping jaw
operated by a man from under a white sheet, quite an
unsettling image! *See picture*

The above Mummer's Play, while weaving together many
elements, expresses the unpredictable yet bountiful power of
Nature, celebrating her cycles, with a bit of good old slapstick
thrown in. Adapt it for plays of your own, if you wish.

The Burry Man

The second example we would like to look at takes place once a year in south Queensferry, Midlothian Scotland. On the second Friday in the mouth of August, during the towns 'Ferry Fair' the incredible walk of the Burry Man can be witnessed. Any townsman who would like the honour of taking the role of the Burry man, must first apply to the local council. The lucky applicant (if you can call him that!) is then dressed in a full body stocking made of flannel. He is then completely covered from head to toe in hooked 'burrs', (these burrs are the fruit of the Lesser Burdock plant 'Arctium minus', a member of the daisy family). In order to spread the seeds of the plant, the burrs are covered with hooks, which catch on the coats of passing animals. In this way the seeds can be dispersed far and wide. There are actually two species of Burdock native to central Scotland and both grow best around disused mining areas and industrial waste ground.) The successful candidate must go out and collect the burrs himself prior to the special day.

As well as collecting hundreds of burrs the chosen townsman must also make two staves from flowers and ferns, which he will carry around with him on his walk around Queensferry. On the day of the 'ferry Fair' the candidate is up bright and early. With the help of his supporters he is dressed in the flannel and burrs after which a crown of brightly-coloured flowers is placed around his head. Once fully decked out he is the 'Burry Man'.

The Burry Man then sets out from the centre of town at about nine o'clock in the morning. In each hand he carries a stave made up from the flowers he collected. He is accompanied by two marshals whose job is to guide him around the town, supporting his arms when the ordeal starts to sap his strength, and thus preventing him from falling over. He is paraded around the streets to the amazement of outsiders. Most of the local children are frightened at first by this

56

apparition of the Greenman. But as the day unfolds they generally tag along behind, being careful not to look into his eyes - the children believe its bad luck to do so. The Burry Man's costume is very heavy and difficult to move in. It is rigid, so the arms and legs are kept straight, which makes walking a slow, painful business. The Burry Man calls at each of the town's pubs and inns where he is rewarded with a drink of whisky, which he takes through a drinking straw. The whisky no doubt helps him endure his task! Sometime in the day he is required to visit the house of the Provost (head of the municipal corporation) where he given another dram of whisky. Six o'clock in the evening after nine hours of slow walking his ordeal is over. He will be exhausted and probably a little drunk, but he has done it! And he will feel elated!

Why is this ritual carried out each year? No-one can be sure for the answer is sadly lost in the mists of time. The walk of the Burry man was first recorded in 1687, but it is almost certain that the origins of the ritual go back a lot farther then that. Folklorists have debated for years over what the Burry Man is exactly supposed to represent, but even such luminaries as Sir Water Scott, were unable to unravel its mysteries. Two principle theories seem plausible.

1. **The Green Man theory**
The Burry Man is the bodily representative of the Greenman the very spirit of vegetation and fertility. He is a stark reminder to the townspeople that the ancient European gods of vegetation are still with us. Good fortune is ensured when harvesting on land or sea when the Green man still walks abroad.

2. **The scapegoat theory**
This second theory postulates that all the hooks on the burrs that cover the Burry Man, capture evil spirits and bad luck as he walks around the streets. All things nasty cling to him. If this were true at the end of the day the poor Burry Man

Padstow 'Obby Oss'

Sue James

Jack In The Green, May Day, Bristol

Sue James

Jack In The Green, May Day, Bristol

Sue James

would have ended up on top of a bonfire, as a human sacrifice. The only sacrifice made today is the physical effort made by the man inside the suit.

The first theory would seem to be more reasonable – the Burry Man is a representation of the Greenman. The burrs are used simply because they are green, they represent the continuation of the natural cycle - and furthermore they need no sewing on, as they attach themselves! While the theory about the burrs 'hooking' evil seems less likely, it is probable that, with similar meaning to the Morris dances, the mere Greenman presence is symbolic of driving away bad spirits.

The Greenman and Mayday

May the first has long been recognised in Europe as the first day of summer. The Celts celebrated May Day by lighting huge bonfires, around which contests of strength took place and much feasting. In those days this festival was called Beltane, or Bealtaine. Beltane is still revered today by modern pagans particularly those who follow the Wiccan path, i.e. witchcraft. (Witchcraft is a religion of nature worship)

The Romans were equally keen to celebrate May and the arrival of summer. Their 'Floralia' took place from the 28 April to 3 May. This was the feast of Flora the goddess of all that flourishes and grows - the trees, vines, and flowers. Although a minor deity she did have a flamen (Roman priest) of her own. Part of the rituals involved going into the forest, felling a tree, bringing it back and decorating it with coloured ribbons, flowers and leaves. This is reminiscent of our Greenman theme. Today you can find maypoles all over Europe - possibly the Roman rituals of the Floralia were the origin of the modern maypole?

61

Hastings Jack In The Green

Dave James

In 16th and 17th century England, May Day was very popular with young and old alike. Garlands of flowers were put up to celebrate the start of summer. General revelries and sexual license no doubt helped increase the enjoyment of the day. Guilds of workers would parade through the streets of English cites and towns carrying elaborate floral garlands. By the late 18th century these pageants were starting to feature friendly rivalry creeping in between the different groups of traders. The milkmaids of London town carried their garlands on their heads. To add to the spectacle, they attached polished silver plates that flashed in the sunlight.

Most notable of all were the guild of chimney sweeps. The attendant boys dressed as lord and lady of the May, capered around their central triumph, a garland of greenery so big it covered the performer within completely. The garland and man inside became one, very much like the Greenman depictions in the churches. The allure of this God-like figure would have sparked deep memories in the human psyche, even though the population was Christian. To 'ground' these feelings and render them acceptable the people just dubbed the figure 'Jack in the Green'.

By the end of the 19th century most of these practises had died out, replaced by more sober customs of the moral Victorians. The huge maypoles of Merrie England were reduced down to smaller, winsome affairs with Sunday school children skipping dutifully around them. The boys who played the Lord and Lady of the May with their capering and mischief making, disappeared when new reforms came in regarding child labour, particularly the Chimney Sweeps Act concerning boys climbing chimneys. The old Lord and Lady of the May were replaced by the May queen and her pretty young girl attendants.

However, the spirit of Jack in the Green is irrepressible and with the upsurge of interest in folk music in the mid 1960, the idea of the 'Folk Club' was born. This interest was understandably fuelled by real ale and illuminated by a splattering of early folk stars, (Fairport Convention and Billy Connelly to name just two). The spin off to all this activity was a renewed interest in Morris Dancing, Clog Dancing, Mummer plays, and local folklore traditions in general. This in turn led to the revival of some abandoned folk customs by local enthusiasts.

Hastíngs Jack-ín-the-Green

The Greenman is various guises reappeared in several incarnations up and down the country. In Hastings in 1979, Jack in the Green was revived by the Mad Jacks Morris Dancers. It seems you can't keep the spirit of the Greenman down and quickly Jack in the Green became the central focus for the town's May Bank Holiday Festival. The festival itself lasts for four days, starting on Friday and finishing on Monday (May Day). The Hastings May Day Festival is very much a folk festival. Over the four days there take place Morris and clog dancing, folk bands and dancing at the Ceilidh. In addition there is story telling, folk appear dressed up as giants, lots of beer flows and the crowning of the May Queen takes place on the Sunday. The main event follows on the Monday when 'Jack' is released from the Fisherman's Museum.

Like the Burry man Jack in the Green has his marshals. These attendants are dressed in green from tip to toe and are known as 'The Bogies' They differ in number from year to year and look after Jack all through the day. The Bogies love drums and the wild throb of their drumming heralds Jacks advancing procession. The Bogies also carry green paint and anoint people in the crowd with a green strip as they process through the town. This is their blessing and is thought to

Bench end, Crowcombe Church, Somerset

bring good luck, those that run away are chased by the Bogies and if caught receive a good green blessing. The name Bogie relates to a woodland spirit also known by the name Bogart, Boggle, or by the more familiar name Bogeyman. As well as his dozen or so Bogies (Greenmen) Jack in the Green has a female consort, Black Sal dressed all in black and covered with flowers. Black Sal is an echo from Hastings past and used to accompany the chimney sweeps in the 19th century May Day celebrations as the chief money collector. Today she is in charge of the many flowered garlands.

After leaving the Fishermen's Museum at 10.15am, Jack leads the main procession along Rock-o-Nore, up All Saints Street and from there to the High Street. The procession then follows the High Street, finishing in George Street where everyone stops for drinks, dancing, and refreshments. The frenzied banging of drums recommences and Jack is off again, along the seafront with the Bogies causing mayhem. From there they go through the underpass, to congregate in Wellington Square. Finally with much colour and noise the procession climbs its way up the steep Castle Hill Road. At around 12.15pm they pour into the castle grounds. There will be Morris dancing music and a craft fair. At 3.15pm Jack in the Green ascends to a lofty vantage point high up on the castle walls, and from there up onto the make-shift stage. Then one last dance from the Mad Jacks Morris and Jack is 'beheaded', setting the summer spirit free to bless the land.

The 1997 festival programme sponsored by Hastings Tourism and Leisure, point out that the Bogies are based on the archetypal Greenmen found in old churches. It is also stated that examples of the Greenman can be found in the local churches of St Clements and All Saints.

Jack In The Green is also a feature on the streets of Bristol at the beginning of May. Here an old custom has been revived. At Padstow in Cornwall the long standing custom of the 'Obby

Oss' continues, a large disk of black fabric is carried on the shoulders of a selected dancer. Songs are sung and a drum is beaten as it travels in and out of pubs, every so often 'dying' and 'reviving', mimicking the cycle of nature.

Practice

If you can make it, Mayday in Hastings has plenty to offer, in terms of enabling you to experience the lively presence of the Greenman. However, Mayday customs abound throughout the British Isles, and there are parades and folk customs at other times in the year, also.

You may like to keep watch in your local paper for events of this description. Some of these may be comparatively recent in their appearance, others are an invention of Victorian romanticism (although who is to say they are not based on older practices?) while others may be much more ancient.

It is a good idea to start a scrap book of cuttings, photographs and your own thoughts and impressions as you attend some of these festivities (and even take part!) so drawing closer to the vibrant and awesome essence of the Greenman.

Finally, you may like to invent your own Greenman celebration, for family and friends. Perhaps a Greenman themed barbecue or party, with a prize for the best Greenman look-alike? This 'prize' could be a proper reward such as a bottle of wine, or more of a penalty, such as having to down a set measure of wine, beer, whisky, mead or other alcoholic substance in a set time. The spirit of Nature theme could be carried into table-dressing, green candles and even a Greenman cake.

Once you have tuned in to the Greenman, your own imagination and instinct will lead you into the best ways to celebrate him!

Chapter Four

A Greenman Ritual

This chapter is essentially a practical one, where you can discover how to make a Greenman mask, and hold a ritual in his honour. This can be fun for all the family, drawing you all closer to the spirit of the Greenwood, in your own ways. The mask-making obviously lends itself to older children. The ritual can also involve children, although you will obviously need to adapt it! Naturally, all ritual needs to be tailored to the temperament and understanding of the particular child. The invocation of the elements may give rise to some interesting discussions. Many children are extra-sensitive and may be aware of things that escape adults. However older children and teenagers can be very sceptical and critical! Please feel free to change the ritual for use by your own family, if you wish.

As we have seen, the traditional form of the Greenman is a sculpture of a disembodied head with no visible sign of a neck. Many of these foliage heads are reminiscent of theatrical masks that might have been worn by the classical Greek players of antiquity. To these ancient actors more was involved here than mere theatre for they took on the personality, of the mask and what it represented. Interestingly, after the player had finished performing his particular role, the mask would be ceremoniously placed in its own special alcove. These theatrical masks were treated with great respect, for they were believed to have the power to change the personality of the person wearing them.

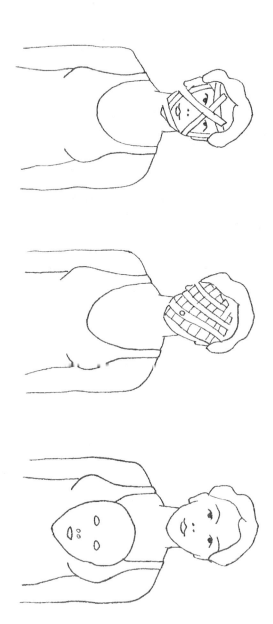

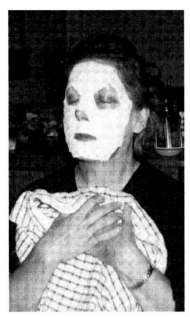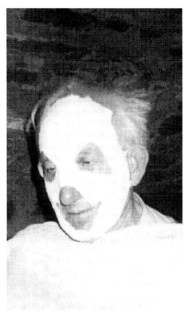

Jan Hardy, Mike Hicks and Rob Hardy having masks made

If there is some truth in these ideas, might it not be interesting to fashion a mask to represent the Greenman, and to endow it with his entire collection of qualities and characteristics? Once we have the mask we can then set about performing a simple drama with the Greenman as the central character.

Making a Greenman Mask

There are many ways of making a mask. The technique we have chosen is by far the most personal, because your own face makes up the general underlying features. This can be decorated afterwards with leaves and branches.

Firstly you will need to shop for the materials that you will need. The base for the mask is modelled from plaster of Paris bandage. If you look around craft shops and similar, you will have no problem finding this. It is sold in rolls, and you should find two rolls are more then adequate for the job in hand. Making the mask really is a job for two persons, one to be the model the other to place the strips of wet bandage directly onto the model's face.

The following is a list of the items you will need:

Your plaster-of-Paris bandage as described

A bowl of water to wet the plaster of Paris bandages.

A jar of Vaseline. You will need this to apply to the model's face to stop the plaster of Paris sticking to the skin, eyebrows etc.

A pair of good scissors.

A towel to put around the model's shoulders.

Once you have gathered these things together you are ready to start. Cut your plaster bandage into strips about an inch wide. Lay them out on your worktable, so that the side with

Altars

the most plaster on is facing upwards. Next sit your model in a sensible chair, comb their hair away from their face, and tie it back using hair grips. Now apply the Vaseline liberally all over their face making sure to rub plenty into the eyebrows - the same applies for beards and moustaches. It is important not to have the plaster sticking to any facial hair If this happens you will not be able to remove the mask without cutting the hair loose.

You can now start to place the strips of bandage onto the model's face. First run your strip through the bowl of water then put it in position on the face making sure that the side with the plaster on it is facing outwards. Wet each piece in turn framing the face first, over-lapping each piece as you go. At this stage it is vital for your model to keep their head and facial muscles still, so no talking! Remember to leave a small hole over the mouth so they can breathe! Piece by piece slowly mould the plaster over their face until you are satisfied you have finished.

Then you must both wait until the plaster of Paris has set. As it sets the plaster will become pleasantly warm. When you think the plaster has set properly, tap the mask to make sure it is quite hard. If all is well the mask can be removed. It will help to loosen the mask if the model flexes the facial muscles, so helping the plaster to free itself from the skin. It is a wonderful feeling when the mask is removed, quite liberating! If some of your model hair gets caught in the plaster it is best to gently free it with a pair of small scissors, be careful not to cut the mask or the model's skin.

Once you have your basic mask, trim it and lay it down on a flat surface. You can now add your foliage - you can use real or imitation leaves, the choice is yours. You can buy thin green wire which is used for flower arranging, in most garden or craft shops. This can be threaded through and around the edge of your Greenman mask, so giving you something to build on. Decorate the mask with acrylic paint, as this dries quickly, plus it is waterproof. You might like to add further decoration such as sequins etc, depending on how inventive you are.

It might be a good idea to make more then one basic mask, in case you make any mistakes at the decoration stage.

The beginnings of ritual

Once you have completed your Greenman mask you are ready to perform your ritual to the Greenman. All ritual should have a purpose. True ritual has deep meaning and changes the consciousness of the person performing it. Your goal is to play the role of the Greenman and in so doing, stir the spirit of the Greenman that resides inside all of us into life. You will then channel this green energy into a bowl of acorns, then at a later date you will give one or two to each of your friends and relations instructing them to plant them in a spot they feel will give the acorn its best chance to germinate. If just one of the acorns reaches maturity it will grow into a mighty oak that's truly blessed by the power of the Greenman. Moat of all, the ritual will have connected you to the wellsprings of Nature in a way that you may find awesome

Before you can perform any ritual you must first create a sacred space.

Temple, church, tabernacle, mosque, synagogue - all these are buildings devoted to the worship, or dwelling place, of a god or gods. Presumably you will not have permission to perform your Greenman ritual in one of the above! As a result you will have to construct your own private temple to the Greenman. A circle is the best shape to use as it forms the simplest ritual space, and being round can be seen as symbolic of Planet Earth. From the shamanic tribal priest, drumming up his circle in the dirt, to the Cabalistic

Magician's elaborate marble-floored circle, amply reinforced with angelic talismans, the circle always holds great power. All circles are equally sacred if the ritual is heartfelt.

Your circle can be marked out with a magic sword or rod, wand or staff, according to the magical tradition you follow. If you do not follow one and are unfamiliar with these practices, find a straight piece of wood that has fallen from a tree and dedicate it to your purpose by asking the powers of Nature simply to bless it. Your circle may also be danced out or built in stones or twigs. It can be marked out with wine, cider, beer, holy water even urine! For celebrations, weddings for instance, it may be marked out with flowers.

After you have marked out your circle using any one of the ideas above or a combination of them, the standard magical practise is then to divide your circle into the four compass points - North, East, South and West. From these quarters you will able to invoke the 'guardians' of the four elements to protect and balance your circle. These four elements are traditionally placed as follows - earth in the northern quarter, air in the eastern quarter, fire in the southern quarter, and water in the western quarter. However, for the Southern Hemisphere, fire may be in the north, earth in the south.

After you have set up your magic circle you must purify it. The most efficient way to purify your sacred space is to use the four elements. For earth you sprinkle salt around the circle. For air you cense with incense sticks. For fire use a candle flame, or if working outside a lit torch. For water obviously use water, although water taken from a sacred well or spring is best.

After you have purified the circle you need to purify yourself. Anoint yourself with perfumed oils which you have first blessed with the power of the Greenman. We have not included this in our simple Greenman rite, but if you so wish you may insert it. Simply take some pure lavender oil and dilute it in carrier oil such as sweet almond, several drops to a teaspoon. Or you may use the neat oil, for lavender is very gentle. After you have cast your circle and summoned the guardians (see the instruction for the ritual, below) then you may anoint yourself on the forehead, breast and belly saying in turn 'May the mind be free' 'May the heart be free' and 'May the body be free'

To prepare yourself basically, in advance, for the ritual you could pray, or meditate on what you wish to achieve. Take the traditional cold water salt bath, beat yourself with birch twigs (which you may feel is a little extreme!) or simply shower thoroughly using lavender soap. Do what you feel is right for you. It is now a good idea to don ritual vestments, for this will help you to 'shift' your consciousness to a higher plane in preparation for ritual. This may be any simple garment that you have set aside for the purpose. Often it is possible to find something that will suffice as a robe in a charity shop, which you should then wash with a little salt and dry in sunlight and/or moonlight, to cleanse it. Likewise wearing nothing at all is just as powerful. Ritual nudity is practised by many witch covens today. There are many people who believe that the magical energies of the human body flow more freely unclad, and, after all, a ritual to the Greenman is a celebration of the natural. What is more natural than a naked body?

The ancient Celts went into battle naked, their bodies painted with woad. They would stand or fall in front of their gods naked and unashamed. The plant woad (Isatis tinctoria) is relevant to our idea of the magic circle and the four elements. It is a cruciferous plant, meaning that it has four petals arranged in the form of the cross. The cross was sacred long before its association with Christianity. The cross, to the Celtic warrior would probably have been symbolic of the power of the four winds. Woad yields a strong blue dye which

Green Man, Jane Brideson

the Celtic warrior would use to adorn his body. If you choose to work your Greenman ritual naked you could perhaps take a leaf out of the warriors' book, decorating yourself with body paint using a suitable green to represent the Greenman. Obviously use a paint that is safe to use on the skin, theatrical grease paint is fine if you can get it. Children's face paint is readily available in most shops selling children's toys.

You can perform the Greenman ritual inside or outside depending on where you live and the time of year and the weather. Remember, there is no occult virtue in goose bumps! Accordingly we have written some advice on outside and inside ritual working.

Indoor Ritual

There are advantages in working inside, and also disadvantages. The main advantages are convenience and privacy. The main disadvantage is not being outside, communing with nature and the elements. Working inside means that you will not be disturbed so if you're feeling adventurous you could throw off your clothes, put on your green 'woad' and perform your ritual in the nude. Witches claim that working magic in the nude helps the flow of their biomagnetic energy, as clothes offer a barrier similar to a cloth draped over a lamp which dims the light. If you feel uncomfortable working in the nude a green robe will be fine.

Pick a suitable room for your ritual and clear it of unwanted furniture. Set out on the floor the biggest circle the room can accommodate. In the realm of magical practitioners, working circles are normally nine feet in diameter or eleven feet in diameter. If you can fit a nine foot circle in your room, great. However, don't worry if it's smaller as it will still serve its purpose. It's nice to have an altar - it will act as a focal point and is a convenient place to set out your ritual objects. A small blanket box is ideal and you can cover this with a

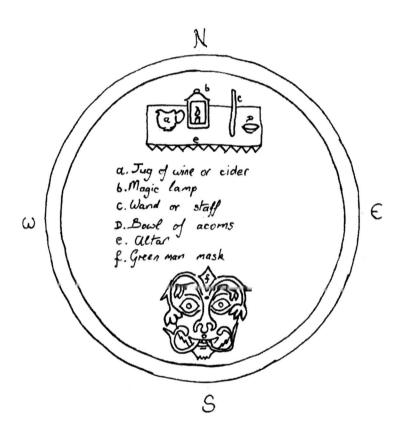

a. Jug of wine or cider
b. Magic lamp
c. Wand or staff
D. Bowl of acorns
e. Altar
f. Green man mask

The Magic Circle

suitable cloth. For the Greenman rite, green velvet would be perfect. You can place your altar either in the middle of the circle or in one of the cardinal points. North is the most usual, in the Northern Hemisphere. One of the reasons for this is the pole star is in the north and is fixed in the heavens while all the stars revolve around it making it sacred to the ancients. The beautiful northern lights were thought to be the spirits of the blessed dead dancing around the gateway to the lands of eternal youth also lead to the altar facing north. Christian churches and cathedrals place their main altar in the east to honour the rising sun, the eastern quadrant is fine if you are more in tune with the Christian way.

Once your altar is in place, it is fun to dress it with flowers, fruit and leaves. The mood of ritual is better served by candlelight rather then by electric light, so place one or two green candles on your altar - their soft light will lend its own enchantment to the ritual. The best time of the day to work an inside ritual is after dark as it adds to the feeling of mystery.

Working outside

The success of a good outdoor ritual truly depends on its location. Please don't just pack your ritual gear and march into the nearest wood! Find your dream location beforehand and visit it more then once to familiarise yourself with the site. Is it secluded enough? You don't what to share your ritual with the world and his dog! When working outside you need to travel light so only take the things that are vital to the ritual. If you decide to work after dark please remember to take a good electric torch with you, when walking through the woods at night as it will be pitch black.

Once there in your fairy dell, mark out your circle. This can be done with natural things that come to hand such as stones, sticks or leaves. Or instead you could mark the ground with

81

your feet - this is called stamping out the circle. It is traditional to have a light burning in any temple dedicated to the light. A lantern with a candle is a good idea as it will not blow out. If you're working your Greenman ritual in daylight, still light your temple lamp as a sign of respect. When you finish remember to leave the site as you found it.

The Greenman Ritual

Things you will need:

A wooden staff

A bottle of Wine or Cider

Magic lamp

Bag of acorns

Bunch of incense sticks.

Holy water

Salt

Earthenware bowl of acorns

Your Greenman mask

Candles (if working indoors)

Bowl or chalice/glass (if working indoors)

Refreshments – i.e. cakes and wine to eat in circle and share with others.

You may also wish to place effigies of the Lady of the Wood (Venus and/or Gaia) and of the Lord of the Wood upon your altar, for indoor workings. Such effigies may be found in many New Age shops – they do not have to be especially intended to represent these deities as long as they seem right to you. It is also fitting to decorate your altar with flowers and greenery.

Casting the circle

Before you cast your circle prepare the temple and set all your ritual items in their place. The salt is placed in the north the incense in the east the lamp in the south and the water in the west. A compass will help you to establish these points although you do not have to be absolutely exact. Light any candles plus your magic lamp. Place your Greenman mask in the north, or upon the altar (if indoors) or propped up on it. Your other bits and pieces can be put near it, or, again, upon the altar. Light candles on your altar, for indoor workings.

Now pick up your staff, stand where you think the middle of your circle should be and close your eyes, breathe deeply and rhythmically until all mental chatter disappears and your mind is clear of thought. Place the tip of your staff on the ground at the eastern quadrant then slowly mark out your circle, clockwise (anti-clockwise in the Southern Hemisphere) with the words:

"I mark out this circle of enchantment as a place of worship. Let it embrace me like a lover, for the Old Ones know me. Protect this sacred space from all the troubles of the world, in the holy and most sacred names of Venus, Gaia and the spirit of the green wood, so mote it be".

You have now constructed the basics of your working temple. If you are working with others, now is the time to welcome them into your newly-made circle. Open a 'gateway' in your circle with your staff, moving it the opposite way from that which you used in constructing it. Take the hand of each in turn as they enter, kiss and bless each other and close the 'gateway' of the circle when all have been admitted.

The next stage is to dedicate your temple. You will now dedicate your circle to the power of Nature under the patronage of the Greenman. First please kneel on the ground in front of your Greenman mask, grasp the good earth with your hands (or if you are working indoors , place your hands on your altar)and say:

"I (give your name) swear to be true to myself and to Mother Nature. I furthermore promise to work with Nature not against her. All this I swear on my hopes of a better life. So mote it be"

This is the first part of your dedication. For the second part you must make a libation, which is an offering to the spirit of the place. Pour onto the ground either cider because of its association with the sacred apple or red wine because of its association with the divine grape. Hold your hands in the air and say:

"*I* (Your name) *offer up this gift to you, O Green Lord, in loving sacrifice. May this act form a bond between us that will span time and space. I am in your heart and you are in mine from now until the end of time, so mote it be*"

(If you are working indoors, pour your libation into your bowl or chalice. After the ritual you can take it into the garden and with a few words of thanks pour it onto the earth)

Next you need to empower and protect your circle with the four elements. If you are working with other people you may like to share the summoning of the elements.

Stand in the eastern quadrant and invoke the powers of the East, saying:

"*I invoke and call upon you, powers of the East, come at my call and protect this circle from any particular evil approaching from the East, in the holy and most sacred names of Venus, Gaia and the spirit of the Green Lord, so mote it be*".

84

Stand in the southern quadrant and say:

"*I invoke and call upon you, powers of the south, come at my call and protect this circle from any particular evil approaching from the south, in the holy and most sacred names of Venus, Gaia and the spirit of the Green Lord, so mote it be*".

Stand in the western quadrant and say:

"*I invoke and call upon you, powers of the west, come at my call and protect this circle from any particular evil approaching from the west, in the holy and most sacred names of Venus, Gaia and the spirit of the Green Lord, so mote it be*".

Stand in the northern quadrant and say:

"*I invoke and call upon you, powers of the north, come at my call and protect this circle from any particular evil approaching from the north, in the holy and most sacred names of Venus, Gaia and the spirit of the Green Lord, so mote it be*".

Now you have called the quarters the next task is to purify the circle with the four elements.

Element of Air (Heat and moisture)
Return to the eastern quadrant and light your incense, then walk around the circle clockwise (anti-clockwise if you live in the Southern Hemisphere, because this should take place in the direction the Sun moves, i.e the power of Light) You are purifying the circle with the element of air. Say:

"Spirits of air hear me, as the incense smoke arises I call upon the Sylphs of the air to protect and purify this sacred space, in the holy and most sacred names of Venus, Gaia and the spirit of the Green Lord, so mote it be".

When you have finished return the incense sticks to the eastern quadrant.

Element of Fire (Heat and dryness)
Go to the southern quadrant and pick up the magic lantern then walk around the circle clockwise purifying the circle with the element of fire, saying:

"Spirits of fire hear me, as the bright flame dances I call upon the Salamanders of fire to protect and purify this hallowed space, in the holy and most sacred names of Venus, Gaia and the spirit of the Green Lord, so mote it be".

When you have finished return the lamp to the Southern quadrant.

Element of Water (Cold and moisture)
Go to the western quadrant and pick up the bowl of water then walk around the circle clockwise sprinkling the circle with water, saying:

"Spirits of water hear me, as the full moon rises over the western sea I call upon the Undines of water to protect and purify this hallowed space, in the holy and most sacred names of Venus, Gaia and the spirit of the Green Lord, so mote it be".

When you have finished return the water to the western quadrant.

Element of Earth (cold and dryness)
Go to the northern quadrant and pick up the dish of salt then walk around the circle clockwise sprinkling the circle with salt, saying:

"Spirits of earth hear me, as the roots of trees delve into the rich earth I call upon the Gnomes of the earth to protect and purify this hallowed space.

In the holy and most sacred names of Venus, Gaia and the spirit of the Green Lord, so mote it be".

Once finished return the salt to the northern quadrant.

Invocation of the spirit of the Greenman.
Put on your greenman mask and say:

"I invoke and call upon you O Greenman of wood and forest. I invoke and call upon you, from branch twig and leaf.

I invoke and call unto you, from long stone halls of lofty church.

I invoke and call you into this sacred space, come in place Green Lord, and come in love.

In the holy and most sacred names of Venus, Gaia and the spirit of the Green Lord, so mote it be".

Feel the power of the Greenman flowing through your veins, energising your whole body with Nature's unstoppable force, just like the sap that flows through those green slender shoots in the spring time. At this time any other persons present at the ritual can say:

"Hail to the Greenman king of the trees"

The Greenman returns to the altar and picks up the earthenware bowl of acorns and presents them to each of the quarters in turn saying:

"Ye deities of the eastern quadrant bless these seeds and protect them in their future growth, so mote it be"

"Ye deities of the southern quadrant bless these seeds and protect them in their future growth, so mote it be"

"Ye deities of the western quadrant bless these seeds and protect them in their future growth, so mote it be"

"Ye deities of the northern quadrant bless these seeds and protect them in their future growth, so mote it be"

Return to the altar and place the bowl of acorns on it. Place your hands over the acorns and try to imagine all the power of the green wood flowing through you and into the acorns. You can do this in silence if you like, or say the words that come into your head at the moment. Otherwise you can use this prayer if you are happier:

"I have made the ancient pact with the denizens of nature. I wear the head of the Greenman. Through me flows the power to fertilize the world. Let this power now flow though me and fertilize these seed with this mighty force. So mote it be"

The energy will have now passed into the acorns and out of you, so now is a good time to remove the mask and set it down carefully in front of the altar. If you are working outside and not using an altar, place the Greenman mask back in the northern quadrant.

You should further ground yourself by taking some food and drink. If working with others, now is the time to share refreshments, sit, talk and swap feelings about the rite and related matters. You could take it in turns to wear the Greenman mask and give your impressions. You may wish to sing and dance. Always leave a little food and drink at the end of the ritual to share with the gods, pouring or sprinkling it out upon the earth

The last part of the ritual consists of formally closing the circle. This involves banishing the quarters and thanking the various deities for attending your ritual. Again this can be shared with your ritual companions.

Banishing the Quarters

East:

"Spirits of East hear me, I thank you for attending and pray you return to your fair and pleasant land, and may there always be peace between us. In the holy and most sacred names of Venus, Gaia and the spirit of the Green Lord, so mote it be".

South:

"Spirits of South hear me, I thank you for attending and pray you return to your fair and pleasant land, and may there always be peace between us. In the holy and most sacred names of Venus, Gaia and the spirit of the Green Lord, so mote it be".

West:

"Spirits of West hear me, I thank you for attending and pray you return to your fair and pleasant land, and may there always be peace between us. In the holy and most sacred names of Venus, Gaia and the spirit of the Green Lord, so mote it be".

Hedgerow Crone '97

Y Brideson

Hedgerow Crone

Jane Brideson

90

North:

"Spirits of North hear me, I thank you for attending and pray you return to your fair and pleasant land, and may there always be peace between us. In the holy and most sacred names of Venus, Gaia and the spirit of the Green Lord, so mote it be".

Now return to your altar or the quarter where you placed the Greenman mask. And say:

"Beautiful Venus, awesome Gaia, mighty Green Lord. We thank you for attending this rite and may we part in love and peace. Hail and Farewell".

If this is the first time you have conducted a ritual, bless you - we hope you enjoyed the experience. If on the other hand you have some experience of magical ritual, may the gods go with you. Blessed Be.

Tortworth Chestnut and plaque, Gloucestershire

THIS TREE SUPPOSED TO BE
Six Hundred Years Old 1st Jany.
1800
May Man Still Guard thy Venerable form
From the Rude Blasts and Tempestous Storm
Still mayest thou Flourish through Succeeding time
And last Long Last the Wonder of the Clime.

Chapter Five

Green Consciousness and the New Age

Might the Greenman have a message for the new millennium? Has our green consciousness grown to the point that we can comprehend the concept that the world we walk in is a biosphere, and that by harming other living organisms we harm ourselves? One of the symbolic meanings of the foliate mask is that man and Nature have a symbiotic dependence.

We are all faced today with many difficult choices. Many people are afraid of science, because it seems to be moving forwards too quickly, gaining knowledge and expertise at an alarming rate without developing the morality to reflect upon the implications and exercise some control. And many of us worry about what happens when science interferes with nature too much. For example can genetic engineering help harmonise man with nature, forming another Garden of Eden in countries blighted by desert conditions and drought, bringing milk and honey to starving of this world – or is it more likely to unleash a nightmare? Too much tampering could not only alienate man further from Nature but also upset its delicate balance, creating the stuff of horror movies in insect-eating tomato plants and sexless larva heralding the twilight of its species. The Greenman himself could pass from the symbolic and god-like realms into grotesque reality as the result of deliberate modification of the characters of plant and animal by the manipulation of their genetic material. Human

St Leonards Church, Tortworth, Glos.

Tortworth Chestnut, Glos.

and vegetable indeed becoming one!

The most likely scenario probably lies somewhere between the two extremes. Nonetheless, all green thinking people need to be vigilant and act always in the best interest of all that lives on Earth.

Concern for the environment is actually a modern phenomenon. In the past people had little regard for nature and countless thousands of mature oak trees would be felled to build the many cathedrals and churches that rose up across Europe. Many of the trees that were cut down and taken away to the saw-mills were never replaced. Today in Britain trees felled for their timber are normally replaced two for one. Sadly this is not the practice in other parts of the world. The quickly-shrinking rain forests are a prime example. Not only is this destroying the habitats of many tribes and species known and unknown (and who knows what undiscovered herbal cures grow in the deepest shadows of the rainforests?) – it will also potentially destroy our oxygen supply. After all, trees are the lungs of the planet, breathing out the oxygen we need to live. This may be seen as yet another possible meaning of the Greenman, who 'breathes out' the greenery, as the green trees breathe out our life.

What can we do to help? When buying something manufactured out of wood, ask where the wood originated and whether it came from a sustainably-managed forest. If you are not happy with the answer, don't buy it, and take the trouble to write to the manufacturers to tell them why

Thankfully, more trees are protected by law today, and some are even listed like ancient buildings. If you live in a British town or city and wish to remove a tree you have to apply to the local council for permission. There are some ancient trees, which have managed to escape the woodman's axe for generations.

96

Special Trees

For us there is one in particular tree that we found truly noteworthy. It is a Sweet Chestnut tree in the estate village of Tortworth in Gloucestershire standing on the green next to the village church. It is reputed to be the oldest Sweet Chestnut in England. To find it turn off the M5 motorway at junction 14 and follow the signs towards Wotton Under Edge. Tortworth is a couple of miles up the hill from the motorway opposite Leyhill open prison. Lookout for a road on your left which leaves the main road and drops downhill. Just when we thought we had taken the wrong road the village church comes into view.

St Leonards Church was first built in the fourteenth century, though it must be said that little of the earlier church remains after the extensive rebuild and restoration in 1872 by R H Carpenter and W Slater. The interior is light and airy due to its white walls and clear glass in many of its windows. There is still some medieval stained glass in the tracery windows dating from 1472. From the outside the tall tower seemed out of proportion from the rest of the church, other then that St Leonards is fairly typical of its kind. We found no greenmen examples in the church, but today it's the Chestnut that's the star.

Reputed to be the oldest Sweet Chestnut in England. Standing on the green next to St Leonards. This tree could well be have sacred connections, growing as it does so near the church and standing unharmed for a thousand years. The tree today has a sturdy wooden fence erected around it, surely not to protect it, as it would not keep a child out, but more likely to proclaim its importance. A few years ago two youths lit a fire against the tree, two men from the village were quickly on hand with buckets of water to douche the flames, and no doubt punish the offenders. So it seems the tree has its guardians. We spent a pleasant afternoon visiting the Tortworth chestnut on a sunny day in August 2002 and whilst

97

St Mary's Church, Painswick, Glos.

Jan Hardy

there we took many photographs of this grand tree. A week
later the photographs came back from the processors. One
photo in particular caught our imagination, for amongst the
foliage there appeared to be faces and fairy forms. This
photograph has been reproduced here, for you to study. It has
not been in any way touched up or tampered with. See for
yourself how many fairy shapes and strange faces you can
find.

The Chestnut is not native to Britain, for it was brought over
by the Romans. Hoards of chestnuts were discovered at
Caerleon. This was the site of the garrison of the second
Augustinian legion known by the Romans as Isca. Today you
can still visit the site of the Barracks and Bath Houses. Some
of the fortress wall has survived, along with an exceptional
amphitheatre. Whether the Romans planted chestnut trees
deliberately or whether their presence is simply due to
dropped nuts remains to be established. Whatever the case,
chestnut trees today are widespread throughout the
countryside.

Robín Hoоò's Oak

One 'greenman' who jumps straight out of legend, is the
famed outlaw Robin Hood dressed in Lincoln green. If you
travel to Edwinstowe in Nottinghamshire you can visit the
ancient oak woodland of Sherwood Forest. There you will find
a visitor's centre offering guided walks along its nature trails.
The main attraction is the 800-year-old major oak. The major
oak is reputed to been used as a hiding place by Robin Hood
and his men. The major oak is now protected by its own
enclosure. Many of its huge branches are supported today by
timber posts. The vast trunk of the major oak is hollow. A
large gnarled opening gives access to its interior, where it is
possible for a man to hide. The major oak is another example
of a tree being protected because of its sacred qualities. It has
managed to weave itself into the Robin Hood story. So in a

St Mary's, Painswick, Glos.

Jan Hardy

Green Man on a gravestone in St Mary's churchyard
Trees in the churchyard at St Mary's
Jan Hardy

way it is Robin Hood that is the guardian of the Major oak.

We looked at the legend of Robin Hood in chapter one, where we noted the possible connection between Robin and shamanism. It is as if we realise, at some level, that trees are portals to another realm of experience as well as being guardians and preservers of earthly life.

Groups of Trees

As well as single celebrated trees there are also groups of trees that are famous. For instance some hills have distinctive sky-lines because of the stand of trees that have been planted on the top. You can see a similar effect on Glastonbury Tor in the county of Somerset, this haunting hill is surmounted by a single church tower, the rest of the church having been destroyed by lighting long ago. Today Glastonbury and its Tor has become a magnet for those seeking spiritual enlightenment, some hills are crowned by trees that serve in a similar fashion to the well-known Tor.

May Hill in the forest of Dean in the county of Gloucestershire is another such hill standing out for miles because of its cluster of trees on the top. Legend said they number ninety-nine, and also that each time another tree is planted one dies, thus keeping the number to ninety-nine. Strangely this odd piece of folklore crops up in other locations, for example the parish church of Painswick Gloucestershire has ninety-nine yew trees growing in its grave yard, each one closely clipped like large green barrow. Like the trees of May Hill the legend states that if additional trees are planted something mysterious happens to keep their number to the status-quo of ninety-nine. Some say that if you attempt to count the trees each time you end with a different total.

As with the single protected trees, groups of trees also have their guardians. These sign-posts within the landscape are often seen but seldom visited because of their location, usually on the top of a steep hill. May Hill, for instance, is a truly magical place with vortex of energy that can be sensed by clairvoyants and a spectacular view from the top – it is well worth the gruelling climb! Many of these hills are on known ley lines.

Practice

It is easy to get discouraged in the face of pollution and deforestation and to feel there is little that you, as a mere individual can do. It can be soul-destroying to go to the trouble of re-cycling and making environment-friendly choices that are a sacrifice, while so many other people aren't even bothering. However, there are positive things that you can do, that will really make a difference.

1 One suggestion is to get your local scout or guide group to clear a patch of woodland. Such activities are usually of interest to the local press and help to highlight the need for care of the environment. This patch of land can then become an area of local interest for wildlife, or a leisure area.

Another activity that you might like to try is to have a tree-planting party. Gather a group of friends together to plant a tree in some suitable place, on a common or even in your own garden. You could do this several times a year on special occasions such as birthdays or anniversaries, or at pagan festivals such as Beltane. Trees can be given as birthday gifts if you like. Members of the group can take it in turns to inspect the tree/s and look to their welfare – for instance some saplings may need to be surrounded by wire to prevent the bark being stripped by wildlife. Each time a tree is successfully planted, it can be toasted by the assembled company and a little of the alcoholic beverage given to the tree-roots, for luck. After this you have the excuse for a party!

Hugging a tree has become a New Age cliché, but there is no doubt that to do this can be very therapeutic and it is certainly worth trying as a pleasant stress-buster. When you need to unwind, find a friendly tree and let it re-connect you with what really matters in your life

2 In this chapter we have given examples of just a few special or sacred trees drawn mostly from our own locality. There are, in fact, countless remarkable trees and groups of trees, all over Britain, and, in fact, the entire world. When the weather lends itself, make a point of hunting down some of these in your own part of the world. This will be well worth your while and if you are at all psychically 'open' your experience will be memorable. Many of the places where you can find such special trees are criss-crossed with Ley lines and natural power lines of mother Earth's most sacred energy, that we discussed in Chapter Two. Their sense of remoteness from your everyday existence can be spellbinding. Take a camera, as we did, along with a notepad, if you wish. Sit quietly and absorb the peace and the impressions that are around you. This will teach you much about the timeless world of the Greenman

The Greenman is not just a pleasant image to toy with – he is a force that is very real and powerful in the subtle realms, and these realms underpin our own existence. Each time we honour the Greenman, envisage him or call upon him in ritual or meditation, we are enabling his force to find its way through, into our realms, and intensifying his 'reality' If we do this sufficiently, is it not possible that his power will become great enough so that the damage to the environment may be halted, simply because more and more people begin to 'sense' him and to fear the outcome if they harm Nature to too great an extent? Perhaps it is time for the old gods to rise up and protect our planet – your respect and awareness of the Greenman can be part of this process.

Chapter Six

Mason and Forester

The Craft of Building Churches

Once the church had found a suitable site for a proposed new religious building, appropriate architects from far and near would submit their drawings and plans for further consideration. When the final design was accepted the work was tendered out to various craftsmen. One of the most important workers was the master mason. His counter-part would be the chief joiner in charge of all the carpentry. Before any work could start in earnest a lot of prepared materials would arrive at the site.

You can imagine the master architect travelling deep into the forest with his entourage to see how the work was progressing. For without timber there could be no new church or Cathedral.

In the forest he would find great labour in progress, teams of oxen toiling to drag the huge tree trunks into the open, already mutilated without their branches. Gangs of men armed with slashes would have made short work of the smaller branches. Axes and saws would rattle and hum through the larger boughs. The tree trunks would then be set out on stretches or saw horses and split by hammer and wedge. Then with one man above and one man below, a huge saw would further shape the wood. Joints and profiles were the work of the joiners, employing chisels and planes. Most of the dressing of the timber would have been carried out on site in the forest. Large wagons would then transport the timber now considerably lighter, due to the men's labours, across land to the construction site.

The practise of shaping the wood on site was similar to the way the stone was prepared. Most of the decorative stone destined for arch or pillar was dressed before it saw the light of day. A good example of this practise can be found in the quarry cave systems in and around Beer, a small fishing village in East Devon. Let us digress to look more closely at this.

Beer Caves, Nr Seaton, Devon

The Beer cave system is part of England's natural world heritage site. It is open to the public from the Monday before Easter until the end of October. A visit to Beer Caves is most interesting. There are guided tours which last about one hour. It is always cold in the caves whatever the weather outside, so it is advisable to bring some warm clothing for the visit. The caves are like a time tunnel - the farther you venture into them the more recent the workings. The entrance leads you straight into the Roman section. There is a small museum in the Roman caverns that houses a selection of stone carvings sculpted by master masons over the centuries. There is also a collection of tools and documents and photographs. In the Roman chamber you can still see Roman arches holding up the roof and the tool marks left on the walls by the early Roman quarrymen. These first blocks of stone graced the villas and towns of Roman Britain. Further into the complex is the Saxon part of the caves which gives way to extensive Norman workings. The Normans cut stone for the great cathedrals and castles of their time. Slowly over the centuries quarrymen delved into the earth bringing out thousands of tons of stone, leaving in its place huge caverns. The sheer majesty of these impressive halls, and massive natural stone pillars supporting the vaulted roofs are overwhelming and remind one of a vast underground cathedral. At the time of the Catholic persecution Catholics worshiped in secret in a little chapel deep in the caverns. This is still to be found there today.

In later years Beer became infamous as a haven for a gang of smugglers lead by Jack Rattenbury. The caves were used to hide their contraband, brandy and similar. Local legend says that the fat of revenue men would be used to grease the ropes that hauled the stone blocks around the corners in the caverns. You can see deep channels cut into the stone by the ropes on doorways and corners.

Until the caves fell into disuse at the beginning of the 20th century Beer stone built 24 Cathedrals, which included St Paul's in London, Exeter Cathedral, Westminster Abby. Also the Tower of London, Windsor Castle, and Hampton court. All quarried by hand and transported by wagon and horses, and by barges from Beer beach. Creamy white Beer stone was sought after, by the masons. When freshly cut the stone stays relatively malleable thus making it easy for fine detailed carvings. Once the stone was hauled out into the daylight it started to harden on exposure to the air. Bearing this in mind most of the carving took place inside the caves, or near the entrance. So like the wood, both stone and wood were first worked at their point of origin. There is no doubt that some of the Greenmen originated from Beer caves. Whether in stone or wood, the Greenman is fashioned from the very bones of Mother Earth.

Working the Forest

Accordingly wood like the stone would be easier to cut when newly felled. Before any tree was felled its profile would be carefully studied to estimate the best use of this living resource. This would be preferably done in the winter months, before its new leaf cover dressed it once more in

A Bodger's workshop in the forest

green. If possible the natural growth of the trees limbs would be used to their best advantage. A natural curved beam has greater strength than straight timber cut into a curve. Numbers and marks would have been painted or cut into the bark. The natural shaped boughs would then have been cut out and lowered to the ground before the tree was felled thus preventing damage when it crashed earthwards. This work would have been carried out in the summer months when the sap was rising; moreover the work would not get bogged down in the mud so much in summer months.

The sight of the forester high up in the canopy looking out through the leaves or framework of twigs to shout his instructions to the ground crew, his rugged face framed with leaves must have looked very like the Greenman! To perceive a human face in this way may be more than a mere passing fancy – it may be a flash of a deeper perception, of the link between man and tree. Arguably, people who work closely with Nature and her manifestations are more open to seeing such connection, although they may take it for granted. After all, the mystic and poet W.B. yeats observed that it was the farmers and agricultural workers who had the most practical experience of 'spirits'

It is surely possible that some of the Greenman sculptures are simply a celebration of the guild of foresters! This is a possible answer for some of the Greenmen sculpture where the face is untouched by creeping vegetation. But however, when roots and stems grow from the mouth and in some cases even the eye sockets, so distorting the face, there must be a deeper meaning.

Bodgers

There was another breed of woodsmen who were called Bodgers. This term is not to be confused with 'Botcher' - someone 'who makes a botch of it' in a clumsy repair! Bodgers lived in the woods setting up a workshop with a simple roof under the trees. Here they would work and live, turning out country furniture on simple lathes, farmhouse chairs and milking stools, which they would sell at the local market. There are still Bodgers working today, if you can find them. In the grounds of Ruskin Mill, just outside Nailsworth in Gloucestershire, for instance, there works a Bodger under a large tarpaulin shelter. (See the diagram lathe and Pic) Could Bodgers qualify also as 'real' Greenmen, or semi Greenmen?

Royal forests for play

Many forests were preserved and some re-planted to provide an environment for a range of wild animals. These animals were in turn hunted so that noble folk could enjoy a day's sport. This gave rise to the gamekeeper whose job was to make sure there was a ready supply of game to hunt. This meant an ongoing battle with poachers. Although the punishment for poaching in days past was severe, some of the braver peasants would be willing to take the risk when their bellies were empty. To dodge the gamekeeper they would dress to merge into the background. The best colours for camouflage were naturally browns and greens. Because of this, could we take the poacher to be a type of Greenman? Probably not. He might look like a Greenman, but his sole purpose would be to kill game and remove timber for the hearth. No spiritual appreciation of the environment was present – and yet the poacher is a representative of the black and ruthless heart within nature that decrees that some things must die for others to live – perhaps the poacher is an unconscious emissary of this force! Many Greenman faces have a sinister tinge, because they reflect this very aspect.

There are many Public Houses and Inns up and down the country called the Greenman. The brightly painted pub signs, which hang outside swinging cheerfully in the wind, invite

110

the traveller come inside where it is warm and comforting. Each pub sign is hand painted and unique. There are Robin Hood types, green imps, giants with their axes or staffs. Greenmen masks and wild men may also be depicted on them. The wild man is characteristically dressed in a close fitting suit of green leaves and usually carries a wooden club he is a reminder of local peoples many superstitions about isolated spots - 'beware the wild man of the woods'! All these signs are a testament to the fact that the Greenman is alive and well in the heart of the British countryside. Even today country people tend to dress in green wellingtons and green jackets, and so forth. The Greenman tradition appears to run in the blood of people who inhabit country places.

Tame Forest

Arboretums are tame forests - a collection of tree specimens brought together by a rich benefactor, usually a keen amateur botanist. The trees in arboretums have been brought back from exotic foreign lands either as a result of exploratory trips or later from lands colonised by the British crown.

The rare seed or saplings were carefully transported back to England by sailing ships hundreds of years ago. Today most of the trees standing in arboretums have reached maturity and are admired and protected in their well-tended havens.

Timber Forests

As the name suggests, these are huge swathes of woodland which are planted with fast growing evergreens, pines and larch for timber. They are quick growing so they bring a quick return. The planting and harvesting of the timber trees would be on a rotation system. Many modern growers boast that for every tree they cut down they plant two more - the Greenman would be pleased indeed! In the past it was possible to see large tracts of land planted with lines of regimented fir trees.

Hopewell Colliery

Today native hardwood trees are planted alongside the faster growing pines. The hardwood is more valuable but growing trees for timber is a long-term investment.

A lot of trees in the past were felled simply for fuel. Surprisingly many oaks fell to the axe to feed the fires of the early glass industry, so many indeed that it was feared that there would not be enough oak left for ship building, which led to the window tax. Despite this, it was the fire in the hearth of countless homes that made the demand for any timber a must. If you still have a wood fire in your home you will know not all wood burns the same, here is an old verse to help you out:

"Oak logs will warm you well, that are old and dry.
Logs of pine will sweetly smell, but the sparks will fly.
Birch logs will burn too fast,
Chestnut scarce at all.
Hawthorn logs are good to last, cut them in the full.
Holly logs will burn like wax, you may burn them green.
Elm logs like smouldering flax, no flame to be seen.
Beech logs for winter time,
Yew logs as well.
Green elder logs, it is a crime, for any man to sell.
Pear logs and apple logs, they will scent your room,
Cherry logs across the bogs smell like flower of broom.
Ash logs, smooth and grey, burn them green or old.
Buy up all that come your way, worth their weight in gold".

Forbidden Forest (Wild-wood)

You may remember that in the story Wind in the Willows, all the small creatures were afraid of the Wild wood, haunt of the dreaded Weasels. People in the past were afraid of the dark forests. They had good reason for these fears, because forests may grow in inaccessible places, such as mountainous

113

regions, or they may be so large that there are no roads to their interior. These wild forests are usually the last refuge of outlaws, social outcasts, gypsies, hermits and madmen. Where would Robin Hood or William Tell have been without their secret forest lair? There was also the fear of the supernatural to deter the careless wanderer. The extensive dark forests of northern Europe were thought to be inhabited by trolls, goblins and giants - and perhaps the spirit of the trees itself the Greenman. Nature is not always benign and trees are not always 'huggable' In Tolkiens 'Lord of the Rings' the hobbits encounter a malevolent tree in the shape of Old Man Willow. We do well to respect this aspect of the natural world, that may, conceivably, be angered by our cavalier and destructive attitude

Industrial Forests

The forest of Dean in Gloucestershire is a good example of an industrial forest. Its particular industry is mining. Mining in the forest of Dean started long ago in the time of the Romans. Most of the early mining was open cast. The remains of the open cast mining can still be found in amongst a tangle of roots and trees. Even in daylight it is a spooky place to be. When the surface material was exhausted the tunnelling began. Shafts were sunk and tunnels were dug deep into the hills. When a mine was worked out it became overrun by the forest and the goblins – so it was said! - would move in!

Practice

This chapter has taken you through some of the practical workings connected with the Greenman. It is important to remember that the things we romanticise today, that we weave stories about and look for symbolic meanings within, were simply the stuff of day to day life for people a little way back in history.

As part of your personal journey to connect with the Greenman, seek out those who work with wood in your locality, such as bodgers. Watch them, if possible and try to gain some understanding of their craft, how it feels to work with wood, what considerations have to be born in mind, how the wood feels and behaves in practice. Do this also with sculptors and stone-masons if you have the chance, for the Greenman was fashioned in stone.

Then try making a simple artefact yourself, from fallen wood. This could be nothing more than to trim and polish a staff for use in rituals such as the one in chapter four. Or you may like to construct an equal-armed cross to represent the four elements, for use in your rituals, and this may be formed from two pieces of wood. These very basic activities will begin to give you the feel of what it means to work with your hands, in the realm of the greenman.

Who knows, you may discover a hidden talent, with the Greenman as your guide!

GREEN MAN MAP

•1

•2

51

38

81

•4
•5
•6
•7
•8
10
•9
•11
•12
•13
•16
•15
•14
•22
17
•23
18
26
•24
19
•20
27 •25
21
29
28 •33 •32
43
42
31 30 35
44
•46
•50
53
48
•47
52
49
54
55 56
59
•60 •61
57
58
•69
•70
71
•68
72
•67
75 73
76
77 78 74
79
80
81 •85
84 82 86
•87
•36 •37
•38
•39
•40
•41
•62
66 65 64 •63
70

Green Man Map

1 ROSLIN CHAPEL,
SOUTH OF EDINBURGH
2 MELROSE ABBEY, ROXBURGH
3 CARTMEL PRIORY, LANCS.
4 RIPON CATHEDRAL
5 FOUNTAINS ABBEY
6 BOLTON ABBEY
7 ST. MARY AND ALL SAINTS,
WHALLEY
8 BEVERLY MINSTER, YORK
9 ALL SAINTS, CADNEY
10 ALL SAINTS, SILKSTONE
11 ST. KATHERINE, LOVERSALL
12 ST. CHAD, HARPSWELL
13 LINCOLN CATHEDRAL
14 SOUTHWELL MINSTER
15 ST. MARY, ASTBURY
16 CHESTER CATHEDERAL
17 ST. MARY, NANTWICH
18 ST. CHAD, STAFFORD
19 ST. LAWRENCE, GNOSALL
20 ST. JAMES LONDON
21 LICHFIELD CATHEDRAL
22 ST. PETER CLAYPOLE
23 ST. WALFRAM, GRANTHAM
24 THORPE ARNOLD
25 SPROXTON
26 SILEBY
27 ASHBY FOLVILLE
28 MORCOTT
29 TILTON ON THE HILL
30 HALLETON
31 LUTTERWORTH
32 CROWLAND ABBEY
33 ST KYNEBURGA
34 BURY PARISH CHURCH
35 ST. MARY, WADENHOE
36 ST MARGARET, KINGS LYNN
37 ALL SAINTS, WESTON LONGVILLE
38 NORWICH CATHEDRAL
39 ELY CATHEDRAL
40 ST. MARY , MILDENHALL
41 ST. MARY, GREAT SHELFORD
42 ST.LEONARD, LINLEY
43 EATON UNDER HAYWARD
44 ST. MARY, ENVILLE
45 HOLY TRINITY, COVENTRY
46 ST LAURENCE, LUDLOW
47 HOLY TRINITY, BOSBURY
48 HEREFORD CATHEDRAL
49 TEWKSBURY ABBEY
50 ST. MARY THE VIRGIN,

LECKHAMPSTEAD
51 ST. BARTHOLEMEW, MUCH MARCLE
52 ST. MARY & ST. DAVID, KILPECK
53 ROWLSTONE CHURCH, HEREFORD
54 ABBEY DORE
55 CHURCH, GARAWAY COMMON
56 ST. TEILO, LLANTILLO
57 ST. JEROME, LLANGWM
58 ST. WOLOOS, NEWPORT
59 GLOUCESTER CATHEDRAL
60 ST. JOHN THE EVANGELIST
61 DORCHESTER ABBEY, OXON
62 ROCHESTER CATHEDRAL
63 ST. THOMAS, WINCHELSEA
64 STAR INN, ALFRISTON
65 POST OFFICE, STEVNING
66 BOXGROVE PRIORY, NR
CHICHESTER
67 WINCHESTER CATHEDRAL
68 ST. JOHN, DEVISES
69 ST. MARY REDCLIFFE, BRISTOL
70 ALL SAINTS, SUTTON BENGER
71a WELLS CATHEDRAL
71b ST CUTHBERT, WELLS
72 ST.JOHN THE BAPTIST
73 HOLY GHOST, CROWCOMBE
74 ST. MARY, BISHOPS LYDEARD
75 SOUTH MOLTON, DEVON
76 ST. MARTIN, GEORGE NYMPTON
77 ST. MARTIN, KINGS NYMPTON
78 ST. JAMES, HALSE
79 BAMPTON, DEVON
80 ST. MARTIN, NYMET ROWLAND
81 ST. ANDREW, SAMPFORD
COURTNEY
82 CREDITON
83 ST. MICHAEL, SPREYTON
84 ST. ANDREW, SOUTH TAWTON
85 ST. MARY, OTTERY ST. MARY
86 EXETER CATHEDRAL
87 ST. BARTHOLEMEW, LOSTWITHIEL

ALSO: ST. MARY, LANGLEY MARISH,
BUCKS;
ST. MARTIN, NYMET TRACY, DEVON;
ST. MARTIN, BROADMET, DEVON;
ST. BARNABUS, QUEEN CAMEL,
SOMERSET

Map by Dark Moon Designs

Gloucester Cathederal

118

Gloucester Cathederal

Gloucester Cathederal

Gloucester Cathederal and Storytelling bench

Storytelling bench, Glos.

Chapter Seven

Calling on the Greenman

In this chapter we take a brief look at a selection of places to visit in the British Isles. You will find a more extensive listing in the Appendix and on the Green Man map.

St Mary de Crypt, Gloucester

In the centre of the City of Gloucester just off East Gate Street, within the grounds of the church St Mary de crypt, you will find a large crescent shaped stone bench with the alluring title "The storytellers seat" We are not sure if it was commissioned by the City fathers or the church. Yet nevertheless on high-days and hollidays it is used by local storytellers who entertain the good people of the city. The seat itself is highly decorated with carvings depicting scenes from fairy stories and folklore. The image of the Greenman mask is used several times, making it the dominant feature. It is strange that the Greenman was given special prominence on the seat, as fairy stories explicitly featuring the Greenman are hard to find! However, the use of the Greenman on the seat is possibly an unconscious salute to his inspirational gifts. Besides, as the Greenman is the very spirit of Nature, he does have a kinship with 'faeries' who are believed by some mystics to be nature spirits, whose job it is to guard plant-life. The Storytellers Seat is well worth a visit if you find yourself in the area.

Gloucester Cathedral

Whilst you're in Gloucester a visit to the Cathedral is a must. The site has been a place of worship for 1300 years, dating from 678AD, when a Saxon named Osric founded a small Christian community by the river Severn. Under the guiding hand of the first Abbess, who happened to be his sister Kyneburga, the settlement thrived.

The next big change came in 1017 when the monastery was given to the Benedictine monks. The first Norman abbot: 'Serlo' was appointed in 1072AD by none other then William the Conqueror himself, six years after the battle of Hastings. The fate of the Saxon abbot is a matter for conjecture! The coronation of King Henry III was conducted here in 1216 and King Edward II was laid to rest here in 1327. The Abbey was dissolved in 1540 and was given Cathedral status by King Henry VIII a year later. In the years that followed there were restorations and alterations that all came together to form the magnificent building that is with us today.

Gloucester Cathedral is home to a variety of Greenmen. As you enter the main body of the Cathedral two rows of massive stone columns dominate the space; their honey coloured stone dappled by coloured light that shines through the stained glass window to the south. Find a pew and sit a minute, take a little time to acclimatise yourself to the atmosphere. It is surprisingly light and airy for such a large building and very peaceful. Time seems to run a little slower inside the cathedral than it does out on the busy streets. Once you feel in tune with your surroundings you can start your search for the Greenman. It will not take you long to find most of the examples. However, there is one Greenman you may have missed, and it's one of our particular favourites. You can find him hiding under the left hand corbel of a small Norman arch situated in the north aisle which leads you out from the main body of the Cathedral into the cloisters. To photograph him Rob had to crouch on the floor!

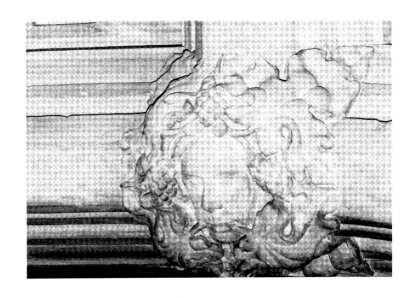

Bristol Cathedral
St Mary Redcliff

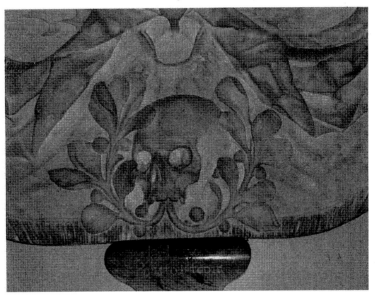

While you are there, do take a look at the cloister, which is a very good example of its type. It is basically a square covered walkway boasting a fine vaulted ceiling with a wall on one side and a colonnade with windows looking out onto the quadrangle on the other. The first part of the cloister you enter consists of the monastic study carrels. There you will find stone recesses. In days gone by monks would have sat in these recesses reading and studying manuscripts. Study areas in modern libraries are still known as 'carrels'. If you walk around to the opposite side of the quadrangle you will find the Lavatorium. This was the Monks communal washing area. A long stone basin with holes cut at regular intervals for drainage stretches along the wall. The monks would have hung their towels in the recess opposite. More recently the cloisters have become famous for their role in the Harry Potter films, having been used as a backdrop for the fictitious Hogwarts school of Witchcraft and Wizardry!

Bristol Cathedral

The Harbour City of Bristol is another excellent place to find Greenmen. Bristol cathedral and St Mary Redcliffe, have some exceptional examples of Greenmen sculpture. Both buildings are located near to the floating harbour, which in times past was the key to the city's riches. Bristol Cathedral started its life as St Augustine's Abbey founded in 1140 by Robert Fitzhardinge. At the time of the reformation the Abbey was dissolved. In 1539 the Nave was demolished and built over. In 1542 the collective Abbey building became the new Cathedral. In 1868 George Edmond Street an eminent Architect of the time was commissioned to complete the work started by Abbot Knowle in 1298. By 1888, the magnificent two western towers were completed, and the Nave was opened. All the great cathedrals have something remarkable about them, which singles them out from the others. Bristol Cathedral is no exception holding a unique place in the architectural history of European church design. The roof of

St Mary Redcliff, Bristol

the Nave Choir and aisles are all the same height. This creates a large hall space called a 'Hall Church'. Bristol Cathedral is the finest example of a Hall Church anywhere in the world. This is something to look for if you visit Bristol Cathedral. Cathedrals are vast buildings, of course. Many of the Greenmen will be located high up on the ceiling making them remote from observation. The dark to dim conditions don't help the process of discovery.

Rob remembers one Christmas as he sat eagerly under the Christmas tree fondling a small heavy brightly wrapped parcel addressed to him. He quickly removed the wrapping paper and there sitting on his hand was a tiny set of binoculars. These rubber clad wonders, were no doubt meant to be used for bird watching. Of course he thought of Greenmen watching! Using binoculars you are eye to eye with the ceiling, housing Greenmen. You will be amazed at the detail a pocket-sized pair of binoculars can convey. We believe one must always be aware of other church users, some of whom may be there for purposes of worship and not stand around surveying everything, like a U-boat captain!

A good camera armed with a telescopic lens is another 'must'. When you capture an image on film it only takes a moment but later you can study the photographs in depth from the comfort of your own home. Yet nevertheless, a longer study of a Greenman in his original location surrounded by the atmosphere the Church or Cathedral might unlock in your mind an inner understanding of his purpose. Another way to record and 'connect' is to sketch him; all you need is a sketchbook and a couple of pencils. As your conscious mind is busy getting the image down on paper, your subconscious mind will be getting to grips with the subtle psychic energy emanating from the enigmatic carved face.

St Mary Redcliffe

Standing just the other side of the harbour and dock complex from Bristol Cathedral is the Anglican parish church of St Mary Redcliffe. St Mary is one of the biggest Parish churches in Britain crowned by its tall spire, its exterior richly decorated. The building gives the impression that it was once intended to be a cathedral. Much of the building you see today dates from the 15th century. The only part that remains from the earlier 12th century building, is the inner porch and the base of the tower. The main entrance to the church is through the north porch - a highly decorated structure dating from the 14th century. I found the porch of particular interest. It has seven arches formed like a hexagon. Students of the Qabalah will recall that the number seven is associated with the goddess Venus who presides over the temple of Netzach which is dedicated to green nature. Directly behind the north porch is the inner porch, which dates from the 12th century, with its prominent black Purbeck marble columns surmounted by richly carved leaf decorations. It was once home to a special image of the Virgin Mary, which was removed sometime during the period of the reformation never to return. After the Christianization of pagan Britain the goddess energy was focused on the figure of the virgin mother to the point that her popularity in the medieval period rivalled Jesus himself. During the reformation the Virgin Mary fell out of favour and many of the Lady Chapels dedicated to her were destroyed. This would have also led to the dismantling of her shrine in the inner porch of St Mary Redcliffe. Today the Anglican Church is happy for people to pray to the Virgin Mary.

It is not unusual to find the image of the Greenman supporting statues of the Virgin mother and Child. We feel there is a certain connection between the Greenman and the Virgin mother and local goddesses in general, linked as they are in the blessings of Nature.

The north porch may have been built to protect the sacred image of the Virgin Mary housed inside the inner porch. The north porch has three entrances one in the front and one on each side thus allowing pilgrims and sailors to pass by the shrine of the Virgin Mary in a procession without entering the main body of the church. There is a stone ledge that runs around the inside of the porch where offerings of model ships and statues from seafarers were once displayed. Spiritual matters were not the only concern of St Mary Redcliffe. In the 12th century the lord of Bedminster Manor one Sir Robert de Berkeley, gave the church a supply of fresh water from a spring located two miles away to the south west. A pipe was then laid from the spring to the parish of Redcliffe supplying clean water to the parish until it was damaged in the Second World War. If you visit St Mary Redcliffe try and find the Redcliffe maze, carved on a ceiling boss. The maze has been lovingly recreated in a local park and flows with water from the Redcliffe pipe – it is well worth a look. Churchwardens and friends of the church walk the pipe's length each year to check on its general condition. This act preserves their ancient right as guardians. We can readily imagine that the Greenman would smile on the use of the maze to celebrate clean water, all springs are sacred to the earth Goddess and are symbolic of her vagina. Her life force flows from her womb to fertilise the land, yet this is a mystery, symbolised by the maze.

We find it fascinating to observe the way all the different elements come together. The church itself is full of Greenmen, symbols of fertility. The Church is named after the Virgin Mary, who is, basically, a Christian goddess. Once there was a powerful shrine to the Virgin Mary placed at its entrance to which people paid homage. The site is supplied with fresh water from a sacred spring two miles away that now also flows through a maze. Combining, as it does, all these elements, It seems to us that the church of St Mary Redcliffe is pulsating with green energy.

Kilpeck Church

On a visit to St Mary Redcliffe in Bristol, which is as magnificent on the inside as it is on the outside, Rob went in search of five alleged Greenmen. Armed with camera and note book, he soon started to spot Greenmen - the count quickly overtook five. As he wandered around the pillars and pews with his wife Janet and granddaughter Caroline, who were enthusiastically helping him in his search with shouts of 'Found one!' echoing around the hallowed building, all this noise attracted the attention of the incumbent of the parish. Asking what they were doing, Rob explained about his interest in Greenmen. The Vicar was delighted by this interest in his church and went on to tell him that there were forty-seven Greenmen somewhere in St Mary's, but even he did not know the whereabouts of all of them. The moral of this little story is 'A squeaking wheel gets the most oil' – and if you cannot find your Greenman, just ask!

As you walk around the interior of St Mary Redcliffe look out for a large whale bone which stands on the head of the Greenman. What might a whale-bone be doing in a church? This is because St Mary Redcliffe has an American connection. In the year 1497 John Cabot set sail in his ship 'The Matthew' to explore the shores of mainland America. Before he set out all offered up prayers for a safe voyage to the shrine of the Virgin Mary. John Cabot on his return presented a whalebone to church. Five hundred years later a group of maritime enthusiasts built a replica of the sailing ship the Matthew, to embark on the some route taken by John Cabot. Her crew also met in the north porch to pray for a safe voyage. The crew presented the church with a model ship of the Matthew, which can be found above the north porch door. Furthermore like the first crew they also presented the church with a wale bone representing the wealth of the fishing grounds found around Newfoundland.

Rosslyn Chapel

Because we live in the West Country we are most aware of Greenman sites near us. However, Rosslyn Chapel, just south of Edinburgh, in Scotland, begs to be visited. There are many legends about Rosslyn and its connection with the Masons and Knights Templar, and there is speculation that the church was constructed to a mystical plan, and that a secret chamber conceals occult treasures. It was built in the 1450s by the last of the Sinclair Princes of Orkney and is the most richly-decorated example of its kind to survive in Scotland from that period. The retro-choir is the most elaborate, and one of its penants ends in the grinning face of a Greenman, with devil's eyes and stems issuing from his lips. On the Prentice Pillar nearby there are many carvings depicting the power of Nature and the sacrifice of the Nature God, upon which we touched in an earlier chapter, although these also relate to Masonic initiation rites (arguably derived from the same source)

Rosslyn has been described in various ways by a variety of writers on the mystical, who regard it as a chakra point, or energy-centre on the earth, in the same way as the human body has chakra-points, or spiritual 'organs' Some have said Rosslyn is the crown chakra. Whatever may be the essence of Rosslyn, Teresa found it a compelling place and was gifted with a very mystical experience after having moved around the church for about half an hour, looking for the most magnetic spot in which to settle. She felt as if her hands had dissolved and her body lifted. There followed several internal visions, of personal significance, and what can only be described as a powerful experience of total one-ness. In memory of this she has the replica of the Rosslyn Greenman, given pride of place above the fireplace!

When in the south of Scotland, it is worth setting aside a day to examine Rosslyn and the countryside surrounding it. The church itself is often full of enthusiasts, with whom you may

134

strike up a very interesting conversation.

Kilpeck Church, Herefordshire

The village of Kilpeck has a very special 'feel' and an air of the
timeless and the peaceful. The Greenman can be spotted on
one of the jamb capitals in the church, beside the Tree of Life
carved in the tympanum of the doorway. Again the Greenman
is found along with another symbol of the sacredness and
eternal quality of life. The corbels all around the church at
Kilpeck are remarkable, containing a wide variety of symbolic
figures that it is fun to speculate about. One of the most
interesting is the Sheila-na-gig – the hag with the yawning
vulva, who represents the womb/tomb/womb cycle and may be
regarded as a counterpart to the Greenman. It is interesting
that this church, like so many others, incorporates many
pagan symbols.

Norwich Cathedral

Moving to the other side of the country, an interesting
Greenman is to be found in the cloisters at Norwich, presiding
over the atmosphere of contemplation and serenity. The
Greenman is an adaptable figure – he is at home amidst
jollity and festivity, in the freedom of the greenwood, in the
hallowed majesty of places of worship and as a guardian of
peace and prayer. Our Norwich example has stems issuing
from each of his brows and beneath each cheekbone. This
four-fold design is reminiscent of the four quarters of the
compass, so important in modern pagan worship, and
associated with the four elements, earth, fire, air and water,
that we discussed in our earlier chapter on the Greenman
ritual.

The above is a tiny taster of the profusion, power and variety
that awaits you in your search for the Greenman, in British
churches. The search should not stop there, for the
Greenman abounds in churches on the continent and may be
found in various guises as far away as the sub-continent of

135

India.

May the Greenman, in all his bounty, smile on you and your quest.

Happy hunting!

Chapter Eight

Meditations on the Greenman

The starting place for your internal journey or path working, is a sacred grove that you will build yourself on the astral plane. Before we describe just how you are going to accomplish this, we would first like to explain a little more about the astral world for your benefit if you have had no practical experience of the phenomenon.

Throughout the years countless mystics and mediums have come across certain supernatural phenomena, of which they have tried to make sense. Through their research a blurred picture or structure has emerged. People across the globe have observed similar phenomena and have tried to fit it into the framework of their own religious creed or magical practises. The end result of all this exploration is a better understanding of this ghostly inner world of shifting energies and intelligence. Thankfully one of the most understood of these supernatural enigmas is the astral plane also called the 'astral light' or 'astral world'. The astral world is the closest to our material world, of the things we can we can relate to using our five senses, touch, smell, taste, hearing and sight. The astral plane is behind the building blocks of the material universe – it both apes and creates all images. Its fluid energies can be manipulated by a thought; a strong intelligent will can mould the astral light into anything it pleases.

A Practical Experiment

Here is a good place to try a quick experiment to help you understand the nature of the astral. Go to the kitchen and pick out a cup or mug that you particularly like. Then, standing it on a table, pull up a chair and start meditating on it. Study your cup at close quarters, pick it up, feel its weight and texture. Smell it - does it feel hot or cold? Flick the rim so as to hear its voice. Place it back on the table and look at it again, what space does it take up in the universe? What energies hold its shape together? Explore in your mind its every mystery.

Now please create an astral double of your cup. Imagine a second cup standing next to the real one. After all the effort you put into making a mental contact with the first cup you will find it easy to visualise the second, although it will fade in and out somewhat - this is quite normal. The astral is fluid and very malleable. It will quickly take on the dimensions of your imaginary cup. When you stop imaging the second cup it will seem to vanish. This is not so, you have created it on the astral plane, although it will now slowly dissolve back into the astral sea, like a sand castle being reclaimed by the incoming tide.

The point of the above exercise is to show you that it is easily and simply possible to build things on the astral plane. The first important thing you are going to build is your own personal temple or sacred grove dedicated to your own development and the spirit of the Greenman.

Setting Up Your Greenman Pathworking

Find somewhere peaceful to settle. This could be inside or outdoors the important thing is you don't want to be disturbed half way through your working. Sit on the floor or if you prefer in a comfy seat, close your eyes, breathe deeply and rhythmically until all mental chatter disappears and your

Birch

mind is clear of thought.

Then imagine you are standing in the center of a large grassy circular earth-working. It is a bit like standing in the bottom of a large shallow arena. Around the edge of the circle are raised banks of earth covered in long grass and dotted with wild flowers and herbs. Along the top of the circular bank stand seven ancient beech trees. Build these images up in your mind. When you are familiar with your surroundings please imagine a pile of cut logs under each tree close to the trunk, to help keep them dry. The trees themselves remain the same - they are unharmed by the presence of the logs.

Visualise a low stone table nestling in the grass in the centre of the clearing. At the foot of this is a discarded horseshoe. This stone table will be your altar.

You have now constructed the basics of your working temple. The next stage is to dedicate your temple. You will dedicate your temple to the power of Nature under the patronage of the goddess Venus. First please kneel in front of the altar, which is about a third of a metre in height, and placing your hands on the altar say:

"I (give your name) *swear to be true to myself and to Mother Nature. I furthermore promise to work with Nature not against her. All this I swear on my hopes of a better life. So mote it be*"

This is the first part of your dedication. For the second part you must now collect the heads of seven wild flowers, from the abundance of blooms that grow amongst the grass. Be true to your first vow and pick just the flower head, trying not to harm the rest of the plant. Set your flower heads out in a circle on top of your altar. Place your hands on the altar and say:

"I (Your name) *offer up this gift to you, O Venus, in loving sacrifice. May this act form a bond between us that will span time and space. I am in your heart and you are in mine from now until the end of time, so mote it be"*

When you have finished the dedication of your temple you are free to leave.

The next important thing to learn is the proper way to leave your temple returning safely to your every day world. Close your eyes and place your hands on your heart and say:

"My will is now to leave this sacred place. As I take my leave may there always be peace between us, in the holy and most sacred names of Venus, Gaia and the spirit of the trees, so mote it be".

As you say this prayer, visualise your temple fading into nothing and the material world coming back into sharp focus. Make sure you banish your temple and thank any spirit you have invoked each time you use it. "This is simply good manners" plus it clearly defines and forms a boundary between the times when you are, or are not path working.

Please note that the reason for invoking Venus is that she will protect you from adverse psychic energy when you are practising your Path workings. She will be your guardian, so to speak. Venus is the goddess of sexual love. Love is all powerful. Venus is also a goddess associated with the colour green, one of her most important gemstones is the emerald. Her metal is copper, which when exposed to the open-air turns a vivid green colour. She presides over the seventh Sephira on the Hebrew tree of life, which is a diagram of manifestation, from pure spirit down to the world of matter. The seventh sephira is also green in colour. The seventh sephira on the Hebrew tree of life is called Netzach, it also has a temple at its heart dedicated to all vegetation and

141

animal life on the planet. Netzach works on an emotional level rather then an intellectual level. So when you invoke Venus she brings all these qualities to your temple.

When you have finished the dedication of your temple you are free to carry on with your path working. The purpose of this path working is to allow you to make contact with some of the ancient deities with whom you will have discourse. This communion will speed up your spiritual development and hopefully give you a better understanding of the Greenman.

Using Your Greenman Pathworking

Each of the seven piles of logs represents one of seven different species of tree. They also represent seven different deities signified by the image of the greenman or greenwomen. Continue with your pathworking as follows

Walk over to your chosen pile of logs, remove one and place it on the altar. Then set alight to it by picking up your horseshoe and bringing it sharply into contact with the stone top of the altar. This will cause a shower of sparks which, as if by magic, ignites your log. The flames will quickly grow and take on the form of the deity sacred to that particular tree. You can then speak to the spirit for as long as the log burns, asking questions and communing. If you do not fully understand all that is said at first, you will at some later stage, so it is good practice to make notes about your dialogue. You will find that some spirits consume the logs quicker then others. Always thank them for coming!

Before beginning path-working it is a good idea to get into the 'feel' of the tree concerned. The following sections give information and lore on each tree. The first pile of logs you visit is from the willow tree – this is evident from the sprig of slender leaves at the top. All the trees represented by the logs will have a similar clue on the top.

The Willow Tree

The willow is often found growing next to water. Whether it be a pond, river, canal, stream, brook, it's all the same to willow- as long as the water is fresh, not salty. The willow has a special relationship with the moon, as does the cherry tree. The willow is one of the moon's sacred symbols. The moon is very important to the life on this planet. As the moon orbits the earth it stirs the oceans of the world, in a way like a celestial wooden spoon stirring the primordial soup! All life forms were created in the sea by the tide's eternal ebbing and flowing, finally to crawl out of the surf drawn by the light of the moon. Life on this planet to a greater or lesser degree owes its existence to the power of the moon. Many people today believe that seeds should be planted and plants cropped following a lunar cycle. In the human condition, women menstruate once a lunar month. There are thirteen full moons in most years, and if a woman counts her periods she will probably find she menstruates thirteen times. Women bleed! Men have built up countless superstitions around this fact. Taboos abound around the world even today, through the irrational fear of the unknown. Why is thirteen supposedly an unlucky number? Could this be connected to the cycles of women and the moon? And could the willow tree have messages about this?

If you suffer with painful periods, you could try invoking the help of the willow tree. Your first job is to find a suitable willow tree. Then take a sharp knife and remove a strip of bark long enough to wrap around your wrist. Strip this bark from a living branch about the thickness of your thumb.

Thank the tree and leave an offering. Don't wash or try to clean your strip of bark. Twist it round to form a bracelet making sure the bark is on the outside. Next time you start your period slip your willow bark bracelet on your wrist. This should help deaden the pain. Willow has natural pain killing properties. The drug aspirin is very similar, and is in fact

143

derived from the willow. The only problem with willow is that if taken internally it will cause abdominal pain. Wearing willow next to the skin, however, is another matter. It acts like a patch, and forms also a subtle connection to the willow tree with its affinity for cycles

Willow pathworking

Invoke your astral temple in the usual manner, remember to collect and place your seven flower heads on the altar as an offering to Venus. Say your dedications to Venus and to mother earth. Walk from the centre of the temple and climb up the bank, there you will find a well-trodden path that goes round the top of the embankment just inside the ring of seven beech trees. You can now easily walk past the seven piles of logs until you find the one you seek. You quickly find it under one of the huge trunks is a pile of grey logs with an sprig of Willow leaves resting on the top. Carefully pick up one of the logs making sure not to disturb the pile too much.

Return to the altar and place your willow log on the top in the centre of your wild flower heads. Pick up the horseshoe and strike it sharply on the top of the altar, causing a shower of sparks. Many of the sparks land on the willow log and fine veins of fire link each spark together like a glowing cobweb. Suddenly the wood busts into flames. As the flames rise into the air they burn a green-yellow colour. The fire scarcely gives off any heat. As the log burns, vapours and steam are forced out of the wood. Soon you are enveloped in a cold mist. The mist draws back and hovers over the altar forming itself into a green man mask made of willow leaves. The more you look the clearer the apparition becomes. Old man willow has become a watery phantom of the greenman half hidden in the mist. His head is surrounded by willow branches and the bluish green slender leaves that are so typical of the willow tree. The face is clear of the mouth eye and nose tendrils seen in some greenman masks. The willow spirit talks of the

144

riverbank and all the life that goes on in and out of the water, the tall rushes that exchange gossip with the wind, or the waterfowl that glide pass on the water. He speaks of the way his leaves gently drop from his branches into the water, as they float down stream they gather together into patterns telling him it is time to sleep for the winter. If you want to know about the riverbank don't ask Ratty - ask old man willow!

The fire has nearly consumed the willow log, the willow mask starts to fade and the cold mist evaporates before your eyes. Close your eyes and place your hands on your heart and say:

"My will is now to leave this sacred place. Thank you for attending spirit of the willow. As I take my leave may there always be peace between us, in the holy and most sacred names of Venus, Gaia and the spirit of the trees, so mote it be".

As you say this prayer visualise your temple fading into nothing and the material world coming back into sharp focus.

Holly

Holly tree could perhaps be more appropriately called holy tree! All trees have to some extent links with myth religion and magic. But our fascination with holly is a special phenomenon. In pre-Christian times the holly represented the second half of the pagan year "the waning year" from midsummer until midwinter. The oak tree ruled the first half "the waxing year", from midwinter until midsummer. They were called the Oak King and the Holly King, forming a pair of twins, one dark and one light. Together they would do battle on the nights of the summer solstice and winter solstice. Each would fall to the other in turn, as the years roll by. Their mystery can be seen echoed in the eastern symbol of the Yin and Yang. (See dia) The Yin Yang symbol is a circle equally divided into a back section and a light section. The way this is shown, the light and darkness seem to embrace another in a rotating manner. The important thing is that in the centre of the dark side is a point of light and in the centre of the light side is a point of darkness. What this tells us is that at the very height of the darkness, light is born, and that all things contain within them the seed of their opposite. The same goes for light - when light is dominant, darkness is born. So on midsummer when the day is longest and light is dominant the seed of darkness is born. Vice versa for midwinter.

So as king of the waning year, the magic powers of Holly king (also associated with the god of misrule) brought merriment and mischief in through the door when the nights drew in. Like the carol tells us: "The holly and the ivy when they are both full grown, of all the trees that are in the wood the holly bears the crown"

Christianity the new religion found out to its cost that the old ways and traditions run deep in the people's psyche. So rather than try and destroy the common people's reverence for the holly, they used it as a symbol of the crown of thorns and the bright red berries represented the blood on Christ's brow. Of course this method of over painting or over laying religious belief one over the other makes it comparatively simple to scratch the surface and reveal older, and it has to be said sometimes more sinister practises of our pagan inheritance, including that of human sacrifice. The rituals of the Holly king and Oak king are still practised today by the growing ranks of modern pagans.

Holly pathworking

Invoke your astral temple in the usual manner, remember to collect and place your seven flower heads on the altar as an offering to Venus. Say your dedications to Venus and to mother earth. Walk from the centre of the temple, labour up

146

the bank were you will find a well-trodden path that goes round the top of the embankment just inside the ring of seven beech trees. You can now easily walk past the seven piles of logs until you find the one you seek. There it is - nestling under one of the huge trunks of the beech grove is a pile of grey logs with an old withered holly wreath on top. Carefully pick up one of the logs making sure not to disturb the pile too much. Return to the altar and place the holly log in the centre of the flowers. You gaze at the altar for a moment, taking in the scene and picking up the horseshoe to strike it across the top of the altar. In a hail of sparks the holly log bursts into life, sputtering and crackling, polished green and berry red flames rise into the air like the arrival of a pantomime genie.

The light and brilliance of the flames form themselves into a figure of a green Father Christmas. His hood is lined with holly leaves and red berries, which frame a merry face. Holly sprouts from his nostrils and corners of his mouth to form his beard and moustache. This greenman is green indeed, the northern lights dance around his head. He brings forth the spirit of the Yuletide season. He talks of the season's festivities, the midnight mass held on Christmas Eve to allow a little sober reflection before the revels begin, the excited children lying awake to catch the sound of sleigh bells on the wind. He tells us of times past, when ancient halls were festooned with chains of forest greenery. Ribbons, holly, ivy and mistletoe were the order of the day, keeping evil at bay, with the promise of renewed life in the spring. Before the holly log is spent the greenman of the holly, asks us to reflect on the homeless, the poor and the dispossessed, and also to stretch out a helping hand in the name of the Holy King. Then with the sound of merry laughing he is gone. Its now time for you to take your leave. Close your eyes and place your hands on your heart and say:

"My will is now to leave this sacred place. Thank you for attending spirit of the holly. As I take my leave may there

always be peace between us, in the holy and most sacred names of Venus, Gaia and the spirit of the trees, so mote it be".

As you say this prayer visualise your temple fading into nothing and the material world coming back into sharp focus.

Apple

"An apple a day keeps the doctor away".

Apples do indeed have the power to keep you well if eaten daily, for a fresh, juicy apple contains just about the recommended daily allowance of Vitamin C. The apple tree itself holds a special place in the history of the world. From Greek mythology to the Garden of Eden, to apple bobbing on Halloween, to love spells, the fruit of the apple tree, the humble apple is there. When king Arthur was struck down at the battle of Long-Down by his half brother Mordred, Arthur's magic sword Excalibur was returned to the lady of the lake. Arthur's body was lain in an open-boat, in which he was ferried to the magical island of Avalon, to be healed - and Avalon was the isle of the sacred apple groves.

Cut through an apple around its waist, so dividing it into two halves and you will observe the core forms two pentagrams or two five pointed stars. The pentagram has long been associated with witchcraft and sorcery. Remember the film "Snow-white and the seven Dwarfs"? It was an enchanted apple that put Snow-white into a sleep of death. Concocted by the evil queen, one side of the apple was poison the other side wholesome. Truth to tell, there exists a vast body of legend and information relating to the apple, and if you wish you could try a bit of research yourself. Tree lore is a fascinating subject, and the lore of the apple not least.

Apple pathworking

Visualise your temple in the usual way and don't forget to pick your seven flowers, plus uttering your dedications to Gaia and Venus. In this path working we will move away from tradition, so instead of having a Greenman to represent the spirit of the apple tree. We will have a Greenwoman. Walk over to the outer ring of beech trees, climb up the embankment and follow the path around the top. You will soon find the pile of apple logs which are marked by a wooden tub full of green apples, blushed with yellow and red hues. You can take one if you like! You pick up a good stout log with green lichen clinging to the surface. Returning to the centre of the grove, you place your apple log in the centre of the wild flower heads. Pick up the iron horse shoe then strike it across the face of the altar stone, as the sparks fly the log catches light, bright orange flames dance on the surface, and a cloud of sweet scented smoke rises into the air forming itself into the spirit of the apple tree. The face is of a middle-aged woman with a jolly smile and apple red cheeks, she has tiny apple leaves for eyebrows. Around her head is a mass of larger apple leaves sprouting from interweaving twigs. Strangely apple blossoms and apples grow together amid the greenery. She talks to us of apple pie, and childhood days when the summers seemed to go on forever. She tells us of her brothers, Vine, and Brother Wheat and like them her bounty can also be turned into alcohol. 'Scrumpy Jack they use to call me I then have the power to turn weak men into lions, and after a long day in the fields bringing the harvest in, I soothe away the aches and pains of the day. But beware! - too much of my golden nectar will addle the brain. My roots go back to the beginning to the Golden Age of man, when my fruit was fit for the Gods'

She bids you farewell as the last of the apple log is consumed. Close your eyes and place your hands on your heart and say:

Elder

"My will is now to leave this sacred place. Thank you for attending spirit of the apple. As I take my leave may there always be peace between us, in the holy and most sacred names of Venus, Gaia and the spirit of the trees, so mote it be".

As you say this prayer visualise your temple fading into nothing and the material world coming back into sharp focus.

Elòer Tree

The Elder tree is usually found by the wayside or in the countless hedges that criss-cross the English countryside, making up the familiar patchwork of fields and meadows. It's not uncommon to find an Elder tree standing tall and uncut in an otherwise well pruned hedge. The reason for this is that country folk believe that it is unlucky to cut down the Elder tree. What started this particular superstition is lost in time. An irrational fear of the unknown or mysterious world of nature is not just confined to the past. Many of the old superstitions are still with us today, furthermore the most seductive and powerful of these are superstitions that relate to trees.

The Elder is one of the fairy trees and if you harm it you will be bewitched. So if it's in the way of the farmer or gardener, best to con someone else into cutting it down! If you cut down your elder tree, other than the expected bad luck you also have the problem of what to do with the remains! The timber is no good for woodworking, true to the haunted nature of the elder it won't burn either. In fact if you try to burn it by tossing it on to a wood fire using a different type of wood for fuel, we've known it put the fire out. So it might not be very good at keeping you warm or building a boat, but the elder's saving grace is its spring-time harvest of lacy white blossoms which can be made into a lovely white wine. Furthermore in the autumn the elder boughs groan under the weight of its bountiful harvest of black-blue berries, which hang in voluptuous tempting bunches. These in turn can also be made into wine with a rich claret colour.

Elõer pathworking

Visualise your temple in the usual way - don't forget to pick your seven flowers, plus your devotions to Gaia and Venus. After you have finished your prayers of devotion to mother earth and Venus make your way from the centre of the grove up the embankment until you reach the path. Follow the path around the top until you find a pile of logs marked out by the bunch of elder berries resting on the top. Choose a log and return to the altar, place the log in the centre of the wild flower heads. Then pick up the iron horse shoe and strike it across the face of the altar stone, the sparks fly but the log doesn't catch fire. You will make it burn! Your temple is an enchanted space and you are the magician priest/ess of the sacred grove! Strike the iron shoe for a second time but this time visualise the elder log bursting into flame. Together with your talisman horseshoe and your magical will, the elder burns with an eerie yellow flame. Due to the nature of the wood white vapours climb into the air. Then the materialisation of the green man head begins. The head is framed in vivid green leaves. From the purple stained mouth, tendrils spew forth, likewise from the nostrils, all joining up with the elder growth that envelopes the head. He looks into your eyes with his jet- black pupils and in a strangely soft voice begins to tell you of life by the wayside. The primrose beloved of the fairies likes the company of the elder and is often found dotted about on a green bank overlooked by ancient hedge. 'Many herbs grow in my shadow some will spice your meat, some may cure your ills some will poison and kill. Old wise-women once rooted under my shade for the herbs that bewitch and captivate the foolish, and heal the innocent. Old man Elder and sly witch like to talk of dark sorcery to pass the time of day. Some think me ugly but they are blind to the pretty fairy sitting in my boughs. I love the way the animals

152

of the hedgerow run over my limbs looking for food. Birds sometimes nest in my crown bringing me news of the world.'

The elder man knows many hidden things, ask and he just might tell you, then again he just may not! The log is now a pile of white ash, the last glow of orange fading fast. As it does the elder man and the log ash are taken on the wind and vanish.

Close your eyes and place your hands on your heart and say:

"My will is now to leave this sacred place. Thank you for attending spirit of the elder. As I take my leave may there always be peace between us, in the holy and most sacred names of Venus, Gaia and the spirit of the trees, so mote it be".

As you say this prayer visualise your temple fading into nothing and the material world coming back into sharp focus.

The Oak Tree
The oak tree is famed for its durability and strength. From barns to cathedrals, solid superstructures are made of oak. The doors and gates of halls and castles were also made of oak, with iron studding to fix the timber together, their strength was phenomenal needing battering rams to force entry, and even then it was usually the hinges and surrounding stonework that gave way first.

A similar door is said to guard the entrance of a magical cave where King Arthur and the Knights of the round table lie in an enchanted sleep. Legend says that when Britain is in its greatest danger, they will awaken and ride forth to save the day. The story goes that the entrance to the cave was once shown to a local farmer by a mysterious figure one morning, whist riding to market in the nearby town of Macclesfield north England. The stranger was desperate to buy the white mare the farmer was riding. The farmer, not keen on the idea of walking home was reluctant to sell. The mysterious stranger waved his hand and an oak doorway appeared in the rock face next to the track. He struck a deal with the farmer that in exchange for his horse he could take from the cave all the jewels he could carry. True to his word the wizard, through incantation, opened the secret door. The farmer entered a glittering cave. On reaching the knights chamber which was jam-packed full of treasure, he filled his pockets with gold and jewels and left in a hurry. The farmer returned to the same spot on the Edge (a name for a group of hills by the village of Alderly-edge near the town of Macclesfield) many times but never found the entrance to the enchanted cave again. He did recall the inscription caved over the door: "Where high magic fail, oak and iron may still prevail."

This story contains many different elements. However it's the magic oak doors of that are of interest to us. Doors are sacred to the two faced god Janus a roman god of the new-year - January is named after him. Doors are sacred to Janus because like him they too look two different ways. Janus looks back into the old year with one face and into the new-year with the other. As we saw in the section on the holly tree, Oak rules one half of the year and holly the other half. The oak king's rule starts on the winter solstice and finishes on the summer solstice. The winter solstice is also the time the Sun Child is reborn, so it seems there is a strong association between the Sun child and the Oak king.

The druids were an ancient Celtic priesthood active in Gaul, Britain and Ireland, respected as magician-priests, and soothsayer by Celtic tribal leaders of the time. Druids held the oak tree in the highest esteem worshipping in sacred groves deep in the forests of Europe. The word 'druid' is believed literally to mean 'oak' or 'oak man'. Today there exist many forms of modern Druidry split into to two main fractions. The first and probably the oldest is the established Druids - Prince

Charles' investiture into this order coincided with his title of Prince of Wales. The interest of this first group lies in the field of the arts, music and poetry plus the promotion of their Celtic language being Welsh, Breton and Cornish.

The second Group is made up from many smaller groups. These are far more interested in their spiritual needs and attract many new age pagans. In many ways the second group of druids, or Gorsedd, are more active in green issues, for instance conservation of trees. If you are interested in working with likeminded people who love nature and trees find your local grove and become a member. The internet, is an easy place to make contact.

Oak pathworking

Visualise your temple in the usual way don't forget to pick your seven flowers, make your devotions to Gaia and Venus.

"*I* (give your name) *swear to be true to myself and to Mother Nature. I furthermore promise to work with nature not against her, all this I swear on my hopes of a better life so mote it be*"

Prayer to Venus:

"*I* (Your name) *offer up this gift to you O Venus in loving sacrifice, may this act form a bond between us that will span time and space, I am in your heart and you are in mine from now until the end of time, so mote it be*"

After you have finished your prayers of devotion, make your way from the centre of the grove up the embankment until you reach the now familiar path that skirts the top of the bank. Follow the path around the top until you find a pile of oak logs marked out by a sprig of acorns. Return to your altar and place the oak log in the centre of the ring of wild flowers, striking the iron horse shoe on the altar top. In a hail of

155

sparks the oak log catches fire, it burns well giving off a lot of heat. It gives off a light white wood smoke, which forms itself into the spirit of the oak man. He has all the character of the greenman his face rioting forth with shoots and branches from all the orifices of the head each lined with green oak leaves. His voice is deep, his countenance is one of great strength. He starts by telling you about the long ages of man, the kings, that have come and gone. 'The hooded druids climb into my boughs to cut the parasitic mistletoe with a golden sickle, letting it drop into a blanket held by a disciple, lest the sacred white berry touch the ground. My forests once covered most of Europe. As the ages passed my strength was employed by man and soon the trees were being cut down quicker then we could grow. Today men seem to be our friends once more and through selective planting are helping us regain our strength. I am the lord of spring! I am moved by the way Mother Nature shows off her charms in a riot of green. Together we herald the return of life after the long winter days and nights. Although I may live for a thousand years each spring brings with it its own special beauty. If you find one of my acorns by the wayside pick it up and put it in your pocket for luck, if you see a spot in the good earth that will give it a chance of life, plant it and we will always be friends.'

With the sound of the wind blowing through the tree-tops he in gone. We thank the spirit of the oak for attending and wish him farewell with the words: "*My will is now to leave this sacred place. Thank you for attending spirit of the oak. As I take my leave may there always be peace between us, in the holy and most sacred names of Venus, Gaia and the spirit of the trees, so mote it be*".

As you say this prayer visualise your temple fading into nothing and the material world coming back into sharp focus.

156

The Hawthorn Tree

The hawthorn is another fairy tree. Being sacred to the fairies, hawthorn is part of the tree triad of Britain: "Oak, Ash and Thorn" Where all three trees grow together it is said that one may see fairies.

Once its blossoms were used to decorate the tops of gaily painted Maypoles. At one time the hawthorns were thought to be witches who through sorcery had transformed themselves into trees. Legend has it that witches and fairies have long danced and performed their rites beneath its shadow. Because its blossom has the scent of a woman's vagina, hawthorn has long been used to increase fertility, and is incorporated into wedding decor especially those weddings celebrated in the spring. In contrast the leaves were once used to enforce chastity It was believed that if hawthorn leaves were placed in the bedchamber of a young maid either in a vase or under the bed it would calm her sexual desires. If carried in a small bag, it was said to be a charm to aid fishermen with their catch. Similarly the charm bag helped stave off depression if worn around the neck. Hawthorn, if formed into a solar cross and placed over the door, would ward off evil spirits and ghosts. Placed in the roof thatch it would protect the building from lightning. In Roman times a small twig was placed in babies' cots to protect them from the evil eye. It is apparent that hawthorn has many powers and is one of the most magical of the trees.

Hawthorn pathworking

Make yourself comfortable, breathe slowly and visualise your astral temple. The seven beeches tower around the top of the embankment, watching sentinels over the green arena below. Pick seven wild flower heads that grow all around you in the short springy grass, and lay them out on the altar top. Place your hands on the stone altar and make your devotions to Gaia and Venus.

Hawthorn

"I (give your name) swear to be true to myself and to mother nature. I furthermore promise to work with nature not against her, all this I swear on my hopes of a better life so mote it be"

Prayer to Venus:

"*I* (Your name) *offer up this gift to you Oh Venus in loving sacrifice, may this act form a bond between us that will span time and space, I am in your heart and you are in mine from now until the end of time, so mote it be*"

After you have finished your prayers of devotion, take your leave of the altar and make your way up the embankment, reaching the now familiar path that encircles the top of the embankment. Follow the path around the top until you find a pile of Hawthorn logs. A sprig of thorny twigs bearing May Blossom lies on the top of the pile. Returning to the little stone altar you place the Hawthorn log in the centre of the ring of wild flowers, striking the iron horse shoe on the altar top. In a shower of sparks the Hawthorn log starts to burn. It burns steadily with a low orange flame. A plume of scented smoke rises into the air and forms itself into the face of the spirit of the Hawthorn. This greenman mask is a fairy faced young woman with white skin and deep red lips, the eyes are bright steely grey. The head is enveloped in a tangle of hawthorn leaves, sprouting creamy white blossom and orange red Haw berries. 'I am the queen of the May! My name is Gaxels, my purpose is to enchant the lonely traveller, on haunted moor at dead of night when the full moon rides the sky like a phantom. My sprite steps forth from branch and twig to take hand with fairy host, to dance about my boughs till dawn. I am sacred to fairyland a gateway from your world to theirs. I am still worshipped and adored across the land. You can see me at sacred wells bedecked with brightly coloured ribbons and rags, each carrying a wish from passers by. You too can seek me out on a moonlit night, ask of me

161

your deepest desires and wishes, leave a gift and if the fairy folk are listening your wish might come true. A word of warning - think carefully before you wish! - it could change your life. If you are sad take a little of me and place it close to your heart. There I will work my magic slowly warming you from the inside with memories of golden times of heroes and dragons, of fairy charms and spring weddings. Be not sad, be of good cheer. Farewell.' With these final words the image fades and vanishes. You thank the spirit of the hawthorn with the words: "My will is now to leave this sacred place. Thank you for attending spirit of the Hawthorn. As I take my leave may there always be peace between us, in the holy and most sacred names of Venus, Gaia and the spirit of the trees, so mote it be".

As you say this prayer visualise your temple fading into nothing and the material world coming back into sharp focus.

The Pine Tree

The Pine tree is an evergreen like the Holly. Pine cones are believed to be lucky, and to bestow fertility – these are often attached to the ends of wands to increase their magical power. The tree itself represents strength and vitality, standing phallic and tall throughout the most bitter winter. Attis, consort to the great Mother Goddess, Cybele, was believed to have transformed into a pine tree after his death, for the tree also represents immortality. Prior to their orgiastic rites, the worshippers of Cybele brought a pine tree into her temple where they decorated it with flowers and threads – possibly one of the origins of our custom of decorating the Christmas tree.

The Pine is a fast growing softwood, easy to work so ideal for cheap furniture, the knotty appearance is its trade mark. You can find shops that sell solely pine furniture. Many thousands of pines were planted on the hills of Wales and Scotland

162

replacing the dwindling stocks of deciduous trees. Many locals thought that their uniform ranks spoilt the balance of the countryside and made the landscape look like a Scandinavian country. Today this practise is not so common, many growers plant deciduous trees along-side the softwood trees. The harvest of hardwood tees is a long-term venture. Hardwood timber being more commercially valuable compensates for the longer wait. However, the enduring pine will always be a favourite.

Pine tree pathworking

This is the seventh and last path working so you should now be familiar with the process of setting up your astral temple and visualising the relative features. As always carry out your devotional prayers to Gaia and Venus, don't forget the flowers. Place your hands gently on the altar and say:

"*I* (give your name) *swear to be true to myself and to Mother Nature. I furthermore promise to work with nature not against her, all this I swear on my hopes of a better life so mote it be*"

Prayer to Venus:

"*I* (Your name) *offer up this gift to you Oh Venus in loving sacrifice, may this act form a bond between us that will span time and space, I am in your heart and you are in mine from now until the end of time, so mote it be*"

After you have finished your prayers of devotion make your way up the embankment to the circle of Beech trees on the top then walk around the path until you find the pile of pine logs marked by a basket of pine cones. Select a log and take it to the altar, place in the ring of wild flower heads then pick up the iron horse shoe and strike it briskly across the face of the stone altar top. The sparks take hold and the pine log burns brightly filling the air with sparks and sweet scented smoke.

The spirit of the pine materialises before your eyes. He has a rugged brown face surrounded by branches, bristling with pine needles. He wears on his head a crown of Pine cones. He speaks to you; 'I am the spirit of the deep forests of the north. I often wear a coat of glittering white snow. I am a friend to the grey wolf that pays homage to the moon. I do not sleep - I am dressed in green come summer or winter. Bring me into your homes when the north wind blows, I will bless you with fertility. I see the blessed spirits of the dead that enter the land of youth that lies beyond the wheel of the aurora borealis. I know where the wild men of the woods live' He goes on to tell of all the use man has made of him, the log cabins that kept families snug through the harsh winters of the past. The mine props used by the race of dwarfs to help them find the treasure in the mountains. Even the humble match to light your candle.' I am all these things and more!' With these last words the log falls to ash and the vision drifts away with the last of the smoke. You thank the spirit of the Pine tree with the words: "My will is now to leave this sacred place. Thank you for attending spirit of the Pine. As I take my leave may there always be peace between us, in the holy and most sacred names of Venus, Gaia and the spirit of the trees, so mote it be".

As you say this prayer visualise your temple fading and the material world coming back into sharp focus.

And so your pathworkings to the trees and their special manifestations of the Greenman has come to a close. Now you may start the cycle once more, if you wish, for each time you will experience something different. It is best to take the trees one at a time and to leave a day or so in between your meditations. If you wish you may record parts of the pathworking onto a tape, to act as a reminder, when you are on your internal exploration.

Your vision of each tree may differ from ours, especially as you become more experienced. Elder, for instance, is often seen as female, explore and enjoy.

Good journey!

Appendix

Recommended Reading

'*The Green Man, The Archetype of our Oneness with the Earth*' William Anderson & Clive Hicks COMPASSbooks 1998. A glossy, comprehensive guide and a good read.

'*The Green Man*' Mike Harding. Informative, accessible and very visual

'*The Enchanted Forest*' Yvonne Aburrow Capall Bann A unique book, packed with tree-lore

'*The Greenman*' (Brewer 1978), Kathleen Basford

'*The Mabinogion*' Everyman 1989 Translated by Gwyn Jones & Thomas Jones

'*The Golden Bough*' 1922 James G Frazer

'*Tree Wisdom*' Jacqueline Memory Paterson Thorson's 1996

'*Witchcraft, A Beginner's Guide*' Teresa Moorey Hodder & Stoughton 1999 A basic guide to working rituals, plus general information on the Craft.

'*Witchcraft, A Complete Guide*' Teresa Moorey Hodder & Stoughton 2000 This is a witchcraft training manual, in essence, which will give you more in depth information

Herbs for Magic & Ritual' Teresa Moorey Hodder & Stoughton 1999 You will find this useful for incense recipes, magickal use of herbs etc.

166

'Spells & Rituals, A Beginner's Guide' Teresa Moorey Hodder & Stoughton 1999 More spells and rituals for you to try out.
'The Wheel of the Year, Myth & Magic Through the Seasons' This is by Teresa Moorey and Jane Brideson, soon to be re-released by Capall Bann. Lots of ways to celebrate the eight seasonal festivals.

'Faeries & Nature Spirits. A Beginner's Guide' Teresa Moorey Hodder & Stoughton 1999 Who's at the bottom of your garden? Find out – one moonlit night!

'The Magic & Mystery of Trees' Teresa Moorey, Hodder & Stoughton, being re-printed by Capall Bann

'Earth Mysteries, A Beginner's Guide' Teresa Moorey, Hodder & Stoughton 1998, being re-printed by Capall Bann

'The Goddess, A Beginners Guide' Teresa Moorey Hodder Mobius 2003

'The Old Straight Track' (Abacus 1974) & 'The Ley Hunter's Manual' (Turnstone 1993) Alfred Watkins – definitive works on ley lines

'A Calender of Festivals' Marian Green Element 1991

'The Druid Tradition' Philip Carr-Gomm Element 1991

'The Witches God' Phoenix 1989 Janet & Stewart Farrar Comprehensive guide to the many masculine forms of deity by these two respected Wiccans. Here you will find deities that link with the Greenman

Organisations

THE PAGAN FEDERATION can be contacted at BM Box 7097 London WC1 N 3XX UK. They have a branch called Minor Arcana for young people. PO Box 615, Norwich, Norfolk NR1 4QQ
www.members.tripod.com/-Minor

THE CHILDREN OF ARTEMIS are a dynamic association for those interested in witchcraft, with a lively web-site that is monitored and so is as safe as it can be made, particularly for young people. Write to BM Artemis, London WC1N 3XX, UK. WEB SITE   http://www.witchcraft.org

Other sites
www.witchvox.net/links/webusa-w.html
www.bookofshadows.net

Artwork
Contact DARK MOON DESIGNS morrigan@mac.com. Or write, enclosing suitable International Reply Coupons or SAE to 'Rainbow Cottage' Clonduff, Rosenallis, Co. Laois, Eire.
www.darkmoondesigns.net

Contacting the Authors
You can e-mail Teresa Moorey on www.westwitch.net. We try to give a brief reply to all correspondence but cannot answer detailed enquiries or help with specific problems – sorry! But anything you say will be borne in mind for future books and will be treasured.

FREE DETAILED CATALOGUE

Capall Bann is owned and run by people actively involved in many of the areas in which we publish. A detailed illustrated catalogue is available on request, SAE or International Postal Coupon appreciated. **Titles can be ordered direct from Capall Bann, post free in the UK** (cheque or PO with order) or from good bookshops and specialist outlets.

A Breath Behind Time, Terri Hector
Angels and Goddesses - Celtic Christianity & Paganism, M. Howard
Arthur - The Legend Unveiled, C Johnson & E Lung
Astrology The Inner Eye - A Guide in Everyday Language, E Smith
Auguries and Omens - The Magical Lore of Birds, Yvonne Aburrow
Asyniur - Womens Mysteries in the Northern Tradition, S McGrath
Beginnings - Geomancy, Builder's Rites & Electional Astrology in the
     European Tradition, Nigel Pennick
Between Earth and Sky, Julia Day
Book of the Veil , Peter Paddon
Caer Sidhe - Celtic Astrology and Astronomy, Vol 1, Michael Bayley
Caer Sidhe - Celtic Astrology and Astronomy, Vol 2 M Bayley
Call of the Horned Piper, Nigel Jackson
Cat's Company, Ann Walker
Celtic Faery Shamanism, Catrin James
Celtic Faery Shamanism - The Wisdom of the Otherworld, Catrin James
Celtic Lore & Druidic Ritual, Rhiannon Ryall
Celtic Sacrifice - Pre Christian Ritual & Religion, Marion Pearce
Celtic Saints and the Glastonbury Zodiac, Mary Caine
Circle and the Square, Jack Gale
Compleat Vampyre - The Vampyre Shaman, Nigel Jackson
Creating Form From the Mist - The Wisdom of Women in Celtic Myth and
     Culture, Lynne Sinclair-Wood
Crystal Clear - A Guide to Quartz Crystal, Jennifer Dent
Crystal Doorways, Simon & Sue Lilly
Crossing the Borderlines - Guising, Masking & Ritual Animal Disguise in the
     European Tradition, Nigel Pennick
Dragons of the West, Nigel Pennick
Earth Dance - A Year of Pagan Rituals, Jan Brodie
Earth Harmony - Places of Power, Holiness & Healing, Nigel Pennick
Earth Magic, Margaret McArthur
Eildon Tree (The) Romany Language & Lore, Michael Hoadley

Enchanted Forest - The Magical Lore of Trees, Yvonne Aburrow
Eternal Priestess, Sage Weston
Eternally Yours Faithfully, Roy Radford & Evelyn Gregory
Everything You Always Wanted To Know About Your Body, But So Far
      Nobody's Been Able To Tell You, Chris Thomas & D Baker
Face of the Deep - Healing Body & Soul, Penny Allen
Fairies in the Irish Tradition, Molly Gowen
Familiars - Animal Powers of Britain, Anna Franklin
Fool's First Steps, (The) Chris Thomas
Forest Paths - Tree Divination, Brian Harrison, Ill. S. Rouse
From Past to Future Life, Dr Roger Webber
Gardening For Wildlife Ron Wilson
God Year, The, Nigel Pennick & Helen Field
Goddess on the Cross, Dr George Young
Goddess Year, The, Nigel Pennick & Helen Field
Goddesses, Guardians & Groves, Jack Gale
Handbook For Pagan Healers, Liz Joan
Handbook of Fairies, Ronan Coghlan
Healing Book, The, Chris Thomas and Diane Baker
Healing Homes, Jennifer Dent
Healing Journeys, Paul Williamson
Healing Stones, Sue Philips
Herb Craft - Shamanic & Ritual Use of Herbs, Lavender & Franklin
Hidden Heritage - Exploring Ancient Essex, Terry Johnson
Hub of the Wheel, Skytoucher
In Search of Herne the Hunter, Eric Fitch
Inner Celtia, Alan Richardson & David Annwn
Inner Mysteries of the Goths, Nigel Pennick
Inner Space Workbook - Develop Thru Tarot, C Summers & J Vayne
Intuitive Journey, Ann Walker Isis - African Queen, Akkadia Ford
Journey Home, The, Chris Thomas
Kecks, Keddles & Kesh - Celtic Lang & The Cog Almanac, Bayley
Language of the Psycards, Berenice
Legend of Robin Hood, The, Richard Rutherford-Moore
Lid Off the Cauldron, Patricia Crowther
Light From the Shadows - Modern Traditional Witchcraft, Gwyn
Living Tarot, Ann Walker
Lore of the Sacred Horse, Marion Davies
Lost Lands & Sunken Cities (2nd ed.), Nigel Pennick
Magic of Herbs - A Complete Home Herbal, Rhiannon Ryall
Magical Guardians - Exploring the Spirit and Nature of Trees, Philip Heselton
Magical History of the Horse, Janet Farrar & Virginia Russell
Magical Lore of Animals, Yvonne Aburrow
Magical Lore of Cats, Marion Davies
Magical Lore of Herbs, Marion Davies
Magick Without Peers, Ariadne Rainbird & David Rankine

Masks of Misrule - Horned God & His Cult in Europe, Nigel Jackson
Medicine For The Coming Age, Lisa Sand MD
Medium Rare - Reminiscences of a Clairvoyant, Muriel Renard
Menopausal Woman on the Run, Jaki da Costa
Mind Massage - 60 Creative Visualisations, Marlene Maundrill
Mirrors of Magic - Evoking the Spirit of the Dewponds, P Heselton
The Moon and You, Teresa Moorey
Moon Mysteries, Jan Brodie
Mysteries of the Runes, Michael Howard
Mystic Life of Animals, Ann Walker
New Celtic Oracle The, Nigel Pennick & Nigel Jackson
Oracle of Geomancy, Nigel Pennick
Pagan Feasts - Seasonal Food for the 8 Festivals, Franklin & Phillips
Patchwork of Magic - Living in a Pagan World, Julia Day
Pathworking - A Practical Book of Guided Meditations, Pete Jennings
Personal Power, Anna Franklin
Pickingill Papers - The Origins of Gardnerian Wicca, Bill Liddell
Pillars of Tubal Cain, Nigel Jackson
Places of Pilgrimage and Healing, Adrian Cooper
Practical Divining, Richard Foord
Practical Meditation, Steve Hounsome
Practical Spirituality, Steve Hounsome
Psychic Self Defence - Real Solutions, Jan Brodie
Real Fairies, David Tame
Reality - How It Works & Why It Mostly Doesn't, Rik Dent
Romany Tapestry, Michael Houghton
Runic Astrology, Nigel Pennick
Sacred Animals, Gordon MacLellan
Sacred Celtic Animals, Marion Davies, Ill. Simon Rouse
Sacred Dorset - On the Path of the Dragon, Peter Knight
Sacred Grove - The Mysteries of the Forest, Yvonne Aburrow
Sacred Geometry, Nigel Pennick
Sacred Nature, Ancient Wisdom & Modern Meanings, A Cooper
Sacred Ring - Pagan Origins of British Folk Festivals, M. Howard
Season of Sorcery - On Becoming a Wisewoman, Poppy Palin
Seasonal Magic - Diary of a Village Witch, Paddy Slade
Secret Places of the Goddess, Philip Heselton
Secret Signs & Sigils, Nigel Pennick
Self Enlightenment, Mayan O'Brien
Spirits of the Air, Jaq D Hawkins
Spirits of the Earth, Jaq D Hawkins
Spirits of the Earth, Jaq D Hawkins
Stony Gaze, Investigating Celtic Heads John Billingsley
Stumbling Through the Undergrowth , Mark Kirwan-Heyhoe
Subterranean Kingdom, The, revised 2nd ed, Nigel Pennick
Symbols of Ancient Gods, Rhiannon Ryall

Talking to the Earth, Gordon MacLellan
Taming the Wolf - Full Moon Meditations, Steve Hounsome
Teachings of the Wisewomen, Rhiannon Ryall
The Other Kingdoms Speak, Helena Hawley
Tree: Essence of Healing, Simon & Sue Lilly
Tree: Essence, Spirit & Teacher, Simon & Sue Lilly
Through the Veil, Peter Paddon
Torch and the Spear, Patrick Regan
Understanding Chaos Magic, Jaq D Hawkins
Vortex - The End of History, Mary Russell
Warp and Weft - In Search of the I-Ching, William de Fancourt
Warriors at the Edge of Time, Jan Fry
Water Witches, Tony Steele
Way of the Magus, Michael Howard
Weaving a Web of Magic, Rhiannon Ryall
West Country Wicca, Rhiannon Ryall
Wheel of the Year, Teresa Moorey
Wildwitch - The Craft of the Natural Psychic, Poppy Palin
Wildwood King , Philip Kane
Witches of Oz, Matthew & Julia Philips
Wondrous Land - The Faery Faith of Ireland by Dr Kay Mullin
Working With the Merlin, Geoff Hughes
Your Talking Pet, Ann Walker

FREE detailed catalogue and FREE 'Inspiration' magazine
Contact: Capall Bann Publishing, Auton Farm, Milverton, Somerset, TA4 1NE